Neil Adams

A Life in Judo

Neil Adams

A Life in Judo

with
Nicolas Soames

WILLOW BOOKS
Collins
8 Grafton Street, London W1
1986

Willow Books
William Collins Sons & Co. Ltd
London · Glasgow · Sydney
Auckland · Toronto · Johannesburg

First published in 1986

Photo Credits
The publishers gratefully acknowledge Dave Finch for his help in supplying the photographs used in this book and to Photosource for the use of the photograph on page 66.

BRITISH LIBRARY CATALOGUING IN PUBLICATION DATA

Adams, Neil
A life in Judo.
I. Title   II. Soames, Nicolas
796.8'152   GV1114

ISBN 0-00-218011-1

Filmset in Linotron Ehrhardt by
Rowland Phototypesetting Ltd
Bury St Edmunds, Suffolk
Made and printed in Great Britain by
William Collins Sons & Co. Ltd, Glasgow

CONTENTS

ACKNOWLEDGEMENTS

This page normally offers authors the opportunity to pay tribute to those who have helped in the preparation of the book, but in an autobiography this takes on a wider meaning. For without the help and support of many people, my judo career would not have been successful. It was due to my parents that I began judo and I am deeply indebted to my father for guiding my first steps and still advising me today and to my mother for giving me unstinting encouragement throughout the years.

I am grateful to Cyril Carter for my first awareness of the scientific methods of physical conditioning and for a friendship that has lasted through a decade of ups and downs; Cyril also provided important basic material for this book. Tony Macconnell and Colin McIver have not only given me the benefit of their extensive judo experience in their joint role as team manager but have also been close friends, again over many years. Important financial help early in my career came from Arnold Humphries, my first sponsor, the Sports Aid Foundation and the British Judo Association, who handled my trust fund. For ten years too, my club, The Budokwai, has given me constant support, ranging from judogi to teaching posts as well as thousands of training sessions. Finally, I would like to acknowledge my training partners, Ray Stevens, Jan Curtis and Caesar Andrews, who have kept me company through years of what would otherwise have been lonely training periods and yet have never complained even after sustaining occasional batterings when my enthusiasm ran away with me.

INTRODUCTION

When Jigoro Kano founded the sport of judo in 1882 out of the scattered remnants of ju-jitsu, discarding the more dangerous techniques and formalising the teaching, he had no idea that within a few decades it would become an international sport. Surviving its introduction to the West via the music halls, its early shortage of teachers and the aftermath of the Second World War, it emerged as one of sport's great success stories of the twentieth century.

This was even more surprising because it was introduced to countries throughout the world in a totally Japanese manner with Japanese names for the techniques, Japanese words for key instructions and even Japanese etiquette – formal bows do not come easily to races where a nod or at most a handshake suffices. But something within the very nature of judo allowed it to retain its original Japanese flavour while slowly adapting to Western physiques and ideas. The basic wrestling concept of taking hold of an opponent, knocking him off his feet and taking him down to the ground to immobilise him is a universal one and Kano, in his judo, balanced a range of techniques with the built-in safety factor of breakfalls.

So, in a judo contest, you can throw with many techniques and be awarded points according to the level of excellence achieved: ippon (ten small points or one full point), waza-ari (seven points), yuko (five points) and koka (three points); and if ippon has not been achieved, once on the ground, you continue until you have held your opponent for 30 seconds, or obtained a submission through an armlock (only locking the elbow joint is allowed) or a strangle. Interest can be found at all stages of judo, in young children, in older people for whom judo is a hobby, as well as those aiming for the competition ladder. And I know, as my competitive career moves into its final stages, that I will never lose that fascination for the sport that has been my life for the past two decades, and I cannot imagine a time when I will not be involved in it in one way or another. For me, judo is life itself.

Neil Adams
September 1985

1

EARLY DAYS

Ever since I can remember, I have wanted to win. It wasn't the ordinary feeling that children have when they take part in their first primary school sack race on a grass track or even the keen determination of a young swimmer prepared to train early in the cold winter mornings in order to make it into the county side. With me, the desire to win was – and still is – as much a part of me as my arms, legs and blond hair. In other words, it wasn't something I learned as I grew older but rather it was deeply rooted in me, an integral part of my character.

Perhaps this competitive instinct is the greatest difference between my public image and the view from inside. I am known as a genial, friendly type who enjoys playing around on a judo mat with children and swapping judo jackets so that I walk around in their mini kits looking like The Incredible Hulk while they trip over my expensive tailor-made Inter-Sport contest jacket which has borne the attacks of some of the hardest men in judo. People see me on *Blue Peter* performing back somersaults on a trampoline or going through other antics for the benefit of the television cameras and I know I appear an amiable Englishman. And part of me is like that. I have never seen the need to act like a bruiser on a Bruce Lee set, looking for a fight at every moment: in fact, I have had only one serious fight in the whole of my life and it wasn't me who started it. I was 16 and about to leave school in Leamington Spa to come down to London to train and a boy with whom I had had some arguments ever since I had arrived at the school decided he just had to try it on. He knew that I had been the Junior National Champion for a few years, but unlike most kids then who still thought there was a mystery in judo they would rather not discover, he felt he could take me on. He threw a punch at me and I whipped him off his feet with my favourite shoulder throw without thinking. I let him go in mid-air, and had he learned to breakfall, he would have landed on the hard floor mildly bruised at the most. As it happened, he broke his arm. No one else has tried it, and in any case, I would go out of my way to avoid a fight. For when you spend most of your waking hours thinking about fighting skills and putting them into practice five nights a week during club training, a backroom brawl is something you can do without.

Central to everything I do is this burning need to win. It is the primary motivating force in my life and it is without question the single most important element in my judo. I remember one training partner – and I have been through quite a few over the years – saying that he had no idea how I managed to keep up the training routines, day after day, week after week, month after month, often on my own, for such small financial rewards and I could only reply that I had no choice. I have never been able to take the soft option of a media career when one beckoned, because of this driving urge to go on competing while I genuinely feel that I am capable of beating anyone in my weight category in the world. But when things are not going well, of course, that desire to win torments me and I have had more than my share of bad times. I have had 11 years of top international competition and throughout that time only once, in the 1981 European Championships in Hungary, did I return without a medal. That alone is not a bad record. Most people would be more than satisfied with that, but this voice inside me reminds me that I have never entered a competition which I did not realistically think I could win. I don't mean just that I was capable of winning it, but that I *would* win it. Even when I was 19 and a youthful international hungry for scalps, I was bursting with confidence. I met Vladimir Nevzerov the Soviet World and Olympic U71k Champion, in the quarter-finals of the European Championships in Ludwigshafen, West Germany in 1977 and I was convinced that I would beat him. Maybe, had I been thrashed, this voice inside me would have been quietened. But despite Nevzerov's proven technical ability, which included a brilliant left tai-otoshi (body drop throw), morote-seoi-nage (double shoulder throw) on both sides and his outstanding jugi-gatame (straight armlock), I took him to time with only a koka on the board. In fact, I dominated the contest and threatened to spin him over with my tai-otoshi on several occasions. He retired shortly afterwards.

And that, of course, is what most people expected me to do following the 1984 Olympics, after being hit by a freak Teutonic wave in the shape of the West German, Frank Wienecke. Even people who trained with me at my club, the Budokwai in London, assumed that I would hang up my belt but within minutes of coming off the mat, there was no doubt in my mind that I would be coming back because, quite simply, nothing had changed. The will to compete and to win had not been doused in the least and if anything, it had been recharged, not out of any infantile lust for revenge (Wienecke hit me by chance with the right technique at precisely the right time) but because I still felt I had not reached my full potential.

Everyone has an optimum potential and while they are performing at well below that level, they will almost certainly be disappointed privately if not publicly. They will feel unfulfilled and flabby, instead of being alert and balanced like an acrobat on a high wire. It doesn't matter so much where the line of that optimum potential is drawn so long as it is a realistic assessment. It may be at the bronze medal of the national gymnastic championships, or completing a fun marathon in 4½ hours. It may be climbing the south face of Everest without oxygen or earning a black belt well. I know good judo men for whom a bronze medal at the Olympics would have fulfilled their highest ambitions. But my highest ambitions have simply been to win the major titles because I know that that is what I am capable of. The fact that only too often those dreams have turned into X-rated nightmares has acted only as a spur. And yet I am still grateful that fortune placed judo in my path for there is no doubt in my mind that judo is my one particular gift.

I may have been born in Rugby, Warwickshire, into the family of an English joiner and carpenter, rather than into a family with a revered Samurai lineage on the central Japanese island of Honshu, but for some unaccountable reason, my natural gifts of balance, speed, strength and a tactical and combat mind exist in exactly the right amounts not for boxing, wrestling (though I have had some success in the wrestling ring as well), tennis, football or swimming, but for the Japanese-born combat sport of judo. And I shudder to think what kind of life I would have led had I been born with the same characteristics, the same will to win and the same potential for judo, not in the Midlands but in the Outer Hebrides.

Rugby, of course, is not known as a centre for judo in England, so there was a certain amount of luck that I started at all. And it was due to even more luck that I continued. My father, Cyril Adams, led the way because he had started learning judo when he was about 25. He had seen an advertisement in the local paper and went along to see what it was like. My mother, Jean, went with him and they learnt judo together for a while until my mother became pregnant with my older brother, Chris. But my father continued partly because there was something in the nature of judo that attracted him and partly because he had always been drawn to activities requiring great skill. He used to play the cornet in the Coventry Band, and he was also very good with his hands – he loved making things and finishing them well so that they looked good. As a result, I was brought up to believe that it was important to see a job through properly, not by cutting corners but by doing it thoroughly. My father saw no point in shoddy work and always felt, in a rather old-fashioned way I suppose, that if you worked hard you could do anything.

My father has shown this in all aspects of his life because though his original trade was as a carpenter and joiner, he studied in his spare time

With my parents, Cyril and Jean Adams; so much of my success in judo is due to them

and eventually became a chartered surveyor. I have always admired and respected him for that and, though many teenagers go through a rebellious stage when their parents cannot do anything right, I have always got on marvellously with both my parents. Maybe one reason for that was because they didn't try to hold me back but as soon as I was ready to move into the big wide world, encouraged me to go.

It was when I was seven and Chris was eleven, and my father was already a brown belt, that he took us along for the first time to see if we would like it. Another of my father's characteristics is that he has never forced us to do anything. I become really angry when I see the way some parents force their children to train night after night or enter competitions every weekend when they really don't want to. My father felt, and he was absolutely right, that enjoyment is the key word for anyone wishing to start judo or any other sport, and it is certainly possible to work hard and still enjoy oneself.

I had been given a new judo suit for my seventh birthday, and like most kids, I couldn't wait to get on the mat. My father took me to the club in Rugby. Actually, it wasn't just a judo club, more of a Martial Arts Centre, though this is a rather grand title for what was in reality a green wooden hut situated in the middle of a pub car park. The senior instructor at the club practised and taught practically all of the Martial Arts – I seem to recall that he was a 5th Dan in nearly everything – but in those days, judo was still very much linked to jujitsu, even though judo had just featured in the 1964 Olympic Games in Tokyo. Most of the moves we were taught, however, were based on judo techniques starting, of course, with breakfall routines. Looking back, I can see that breakfall practice is crucial as you cannot start to work well on throwing techniques with a partner if you are afraid of being thrown, but I am sure that many promising sportsmen are lost to judo because of the boring way that breakfalls are so often taught. My father used to encourage Chris and me to vary our training by including some basic gymnastic skills such as handstands, cartwheels and eventually handsprings, though it wasn't until a lot later in my judo career that I became aware of how very important these would become to me.

After about a year, we moved to Leamington Spa, and my father, realising that I had some talent, felt that an established judo club was needed. Thus Coventry judo club was selected, and has remained my spritual home to this very day. I will never forget my first day on that judo mat. Having come from my little green hut full of confidence, the last thing I expected was to get completely thrashed. But I was bounced from corner to corner and I quickly learned that it was not an experience I relished. Far from putting me off the sport, it helped me develop a strong resolve to alter this state of affairs as quickly as possible, which I did. A few months later, I entered a contest and won my first medal – not, however, for winning, but for exhibiting the best style. I really think they gave it to me for being the smallest and pluckiest of the contestants on that day. The following year, 1967, saw my very first contest-earned medal, a victory in the Midland Area Tiny Tots Championships, which I won in 1968 as well.

However, 1968 was more important for the fact that I found myself for the first time on the mat of Crystal Palace National Sports Centre, competing in the Junior National Championships. The event, the size of the place, the lights and just about everything else overawed me and for the first time I felt terribly nervous so it wasn't surprising that I lost to one of the Hawkins twins whom I fought right through my junior career. For the first and only time, my father told me off, not because I lost, but because I made the same mistake twice. I got caught on the ground, managed to wriggle out of the hold, and then got caught again in exactly the same way, and this time held for a score. It infuriated my father because it happened twice, but it also angered me, because I felt I was technically superior, even if I didn't have the strength at the time. I was giving away a lot of weight – I had asked my father to let me diet in order to stay in the Tiny Tots category, but he wouldn't let me, rightly, of course. I was always short and my parents thought there might be something wrong with me because I was growing so slowly. But in the end, it was just a question of technique. I beat the boy the following year, and was never beaten by either of the Hawkins brothers after that.

I beat the boy the following year when I won my first junior national title at 5 stone 8 pounds. I was still nervous, but I had improved. I fought a boy called Popodopoulous in the final on decision, but I had won all my fights with ippon on the way through. I particularly remember the semi-final fight because I met Chris Bowles who was to become a respected opponent, a training partner and a friend – we even went to Japan together. I beat him with two waza-aris, throwing him with morote-seoi-nage which was practically all I did then. I was a typical junior fighter, in that I had only one throw – morote-seoi. If I couldn't throw my opponents with that, I didn't really think of trying anything else. I wasn't inept at groundwork and I held some kids down. But unless the hold went on immediately, I would just stand up and try to throw.

This was very much the pattern of the next few years. We had had some changes at home for my father had run a pub – the Woodland Tavern in a rough part of Leamington – for a time and they hated it, so he began working for Coventry Corporation. After winning my first Nationals, I did one extra night's judo practice a week, bringing it up to a total of four or five nights, and I thought that that was taking it seriously but times were very different then. I wasn't doing any of the complementary fitness training that kids do now and just did my judo. But even at this age, when I was 11 and 12, I used to dream of one day being not just National Champion but World Champion. Consequently, my schoolwork suffered and all my reports used to say: 'If Neil could put an eighth of what he puts into judo into his schoolwork, he could be doing very well.' And I know this was true, because I am reasonably bright.

However, Britain is very slow to change its educational system. I think it is a terrible shame that so many sportsmen end up with good sports careers but with little to show academically because the existing system makes very little provision for special sports facilities. There are specialist music schools which manage to produce curricula combining the necessary hours of practice with a more flexible but still significant academic timetable, so there is no real reason why the same should not be introduced for those with outstanding sports skills. Now, when I see young talented judo players coming through, I try to impress on them that they must not neglect their schoolwork, but words like that cannot really compete with the glint of the pots and medals handed out at competitions.

Curiously, there weren't as many pots and medals lining the walls of my room as those of my contemporaries but that was because my father severely restricted the number of competitions I entered. For a long time, I couldn't understand why I was entered only for the Midland Area events, the National Competitions and a few others but, in retrospect, I can see my father was being extremely shrewd. He had seen so many young sportsmen start off by winning everything in sight, only to give up under the pressure of it all – most of the pressure coming from the parents – that he didn't want to repeat the same mistake with me. He wanted me to retain a hunger for competition and organised my schedule around no more than six a year. So the competitions I did enter were special events in the Adams household and with Chris competing and often bringing home medals – we both won junior national titles in 1972 – competitions became major family outings.

I won the National Junior title five years in succession, from 1969 to 1973, and it proved invaluable experience. I always wanted to stand upright and throw my opponents with a devastating morote-seoi-nage but I don't really know why. It may have been the fruit of that seed planted so

---

My fifth consecutive national title was won in the U60k in 1973 with W. Shields (Scotland) taking the silver and C. Brace (NHC) and C. Morgan (South) the bronzes

early in my career – the winning of my first medal for style. Probably I just wanted to play to the crowd and I learnt to do that as well. Victory, I am afraid, taught me to be rather cocky and cheeky in my early teens. I may have used it as a front at first, to protect and hide my burning desire to win, but after a while, it became too much a part of my personality though as a teenager fighting against the best men in the world, it may have given me that miraculous super-confidence which is the preserve of youth. But in my early teens, I must have been altogether rather objectionable.

However, I never took liberties with my father. He is very placid, though my mother has a fiery temper, and I have known him to hit me only once. I was twelve and I pinched a Mars bar from a shop near where we lived but I was sure I hadn't been seen. When I went home though, my father was standing in the hall waiting for me; the woman in the shop who knew us had seen me and had immediately telephoned him. He asked me directly if I had taken a Mars bar, and as I started to deny it, he hit me so hard that he nearly knocked my head off my shoulders. I remember reeling against the wall. But we have been firm friends ever since; it was just that he couldn't stand the act of stealing.

Other lessons were learned at this time, including the importance of learning from mistakes, and fast. In the 1972 Nationals at Crystal Palace, I lost my fourth fight on a split decision and I thought that that was the end of my run of titles. However, my father explained that because of the pool system, I could still come through. I clearly remember him adding, 'But you will have to fight better than that, you know.' Perhaps I was just coasting because of my past wins and the shock of losing pushed me up a gear, or perhaps I really did learn quickly where the weaknesses of that particular opponent lay. But I fought through to the final where I met that same boy again and this time I beat him easily.

It then became clear to me that there are some opponents whom it is not possible to throw in a nice, clear technique – those opponents who just come in and fall on their face or who double up in defence – and at the time I just didn't have the technical ability to do what needed to be done: take them on the ground. But the standard of junior judo then, the type of training we did and the level of teaching, was simply lower than that which exists today. We thought we were being serious but we really didn't have a clue; there was no junior squad system at the time, so the National Championships at Crystal Palace was simply the pinnacle of judo achievement for us. I did work hard, or what I thought was hard, but I was relying mainly on some natural talent and my determination to win.

It was in the middle of this run of titles that I suffered my first major injury. One of the dangers of morote-seoi-nage, especially the way it is done as a junior where speed into the throw rather than breaking your opponent's balance is the crucial element, is that the most instinctive defence is to wrench the attacker backwards, and this began to happen to me more often. I would have the occasional week off, and then return to the mat, until the next time. When I was about 13, I was fighting in a contest in the Midlands and was pulled back so severely that I couldn't continue. My father withdrew me from the competition and told me categorically I had to stop doing the throw. At the time, it seemed a bit like the end of the world to me because the throw came naturally to me and I couldn't really perform anything else to anywhere near the same standard. But my father insisted. The next time we went to the Coventry Judo Club to practise, he stopped me outside the door, looked me straight in the eyes, and said, 'If I see you doing morote-seoi-nage, I will really be furious with you. Either you change, or you pack in judo.' I just looked up at him and asked rather desperately, 'What else can I do?' 'Try tai-otoshi,' he replied immediately.

It was a turning point in my career. At first, I couldn't throw anyone with tai-otoshi. It felt awkward and uncontrolled and seemed to lack the spectacular qualities of my beloved morote-seoi-nage. Perhaps for as long as a year, I relied almost totally on kouchi-gari in competition because my tai-otoshi simply wasn't effective. But I didn't think of giving up for two reasons. First of all, I am a fighter and like challenges, or more accurately, I like the feeling of overcoming them, even though it may take time. Secondly, I was now committed to making my mark through judo.

I had never really wavered from the sport but a few months before I had had a momentary flirtation with football, which is a game I still love. I played quite well when I was 12 and earned a place in the mid-Warwickshire side. I played forward and was greedy for possession and for goals as the urge to win was just as evident on the football field as it was on the judo mat. I was all set to have a trial for Coventry City Youth Team when an incident decided my future for me. I remember playing against the City Youth Team, and coming across a boy who was just a little bit special. I realised that there was no way I was going to be that good so I stuck to judo. It seemed such a minor decision at the time, but what major consequences it had! I sometimes wonder what would have happened if, by some chance, I had scored on that day, and in the ensuing euphoria, pressed ahead with soccer trials . . .

My now total commitment to judo meant, first and foremost, work on the tai-otoshi. Unlike the morote-seoi-nage, it didn't come easily, but now it is the central throw in my whole tachi-waza armoury, the throw to which I connect almost all my other techniques – uchi-mata, osoto-gari, kouchi-gari, kosoto-gari and even tomoe-nage – and the throw with which I have had greatest success. Gamba, Dvoinikov, and Kase are among the leading internationals to have fallen prey to it and the number of lesser figures who have been caught by it are countless.

So adversity sometimes does bring special rewards. I was intrigued to hear that much the same thing happened to Katsuhiko Kashiwazaki, the 65-kilo Japanese fighter who won his World Championship title the day after me in Maastricht, and who taught for a year at the Budokwai between 1983–84. He is renowned for his groundwork, but his early successes came from his morote-seoi-nage until injury – in his case a broken elbow – forced him to review his judo completely. He developed ashi-waza and tomoe-nage and completely switched the emphasis of his judo from standing work to groundwork and only then went on to win five All-Japan weight category titles and the world title in 1981.

My early teens were marked by competition success but at the same time I was gradually moving up through the grading system. When I was 14, I decided to try for a senior brown belt even though I was only 50 kilos. Although it was important to me at the time, I don't remember much about it now, except that it was in Derby, and my opponents were all much bigger. I remember one giant becoming increasingly irritated and then angry because he couldn't throw me even though he must have been about 100 kilos. I couldn't throw him either, in fact I couldn't even move him, but eventually I won my ten points because he grew so frustrated that he just yelled at me 'Get lost' and slung me into a load of chairs. He was disqualified, of course, and I threw the others, so my senior brown belt was confirmed.

A year later, when I weighed about 55 kilos, I went for my black belt and it seemed relatively easy. I won my first two preliminaries, and then went straight through the line-up of four opponents of different sizes. It has been said that the first Dan, which is the first time you wear a black belt, is the most thrilling to achieve of all the grades, and it was certainly important to me. People didn't believe I was a black belt because I was only a boy, and I think now that I should have been forced to wait until I was 16. But at 15, life is much simpler. I had earned it, so I should, by rights, wear it. And I did, with pride.

By this time, I had begun to look seriously at the young men's competition world and the senior ranks dominated by Brian Jacks, Dave Starbrook and Keith Remfrey, but particularly at my next step, the Espoir level, which catered for the 16- to 18-year-olds. The difference in body strength between most 15-year-olds and a trained fighting man in his middle twenties is enormous and the Espoir level was created specially to allow time for the physique to harden and mature before pitching in eager competitors at a top level. I entered my first Espoir championship when I was 15, in 1973, and came second to a boy called 'Porky' Waters. I remember nothing about the event – I think I lost on a decision or a koka – except that I realised I was now no longer the automatic choice for the event I was really aiming at which was to have been my first international, the Espoir Europeans being held in Tel Aviv in November. So I took the somewhat bold step of ringing up Syd Hoare, the chief instructor at the Budokwai who was then also in charge of the Espoir squad, and introducing myself. I bluntly asked him if he had picked the team for the Europeans yet and he said he hadn't. 'If I were you, I would pick me,' I said as I was that kind of kid, cocky and arrogant. 'If you pick me, I will win a medal for you.' And I really meant it. He said he would think about it. The conversation did not end there because I then asked him whether he could help me if I came down to London, and he said he would and that he knew of a house where I could stay.

Suddenly, the direction in which my future lay became clearer. I had already made the decision to concentrate on judo rather than to stay on at school but this crystallised matters. After a week or so, Syd rang me to say that I was in the team, and I couldn't believe it. I attended a couple of squad training sessions but apart from that, I didn't prepare specially. Also, I couldn't celebrate my success because I was too busy trying to lose weight. I was dieting furiously which was absolute madness really because I should have gone up to the next weight category rather than force myself down to U58k. But Chris Bowles was also in the team and fighting at the weight above, so it was convenient for me to go down, especially as I had no idea of the correct and safe way of losing weight. I thought an empty stomach just meant I was getting near the weight.

The Espoir European Championships in November 1974 could have been something of an anti-climax because, for political reasons, the Russians decided not to take part but to me it was still the biggest competition I had ever entered. It was amazing to see all those faces for the first time, faces such as that of Ezio Gamba (he eventually lost to Chris Bowles in the final) who I would fight many times during my career. Although I obviously supported Chris in that fight, I couldn't help but be impressed by the obvious agility of Gamba's judo brain. I was giving away nearly two years to most of my opponents but I still went straight through to the final without much difficulty, usually winning by combining ouchi-gari and drop ippon-seoi-nage. I found it rather unbelievable, and with two other gold medals in the English camp – one from Chris Bowles and another from the heavyweight, Alex Ives – the atmosphere was really

My first national title in the Espoir division, the 1974 Young Men's Championships, was held just a few months and a haircut after my last junior title. I was still a brown belt. With me on the podium is: B. Morrison (NHC), silver; J. Nixon (North East); and J. Anderson (London)

fantastic. But with the competition over, the fun was only just beginning – for some. I may have been an able contest player but in other areas I was still a naive 16-year-old from the Midlands away on my first major trip abroad, and it was decided that my education should be helped along apace. In short, without being aware that I was being set up, I was introduced to a young lady whose business it was to broaden the education of boys like me. As soon as I realised what was happening, I managed to break away and set off hotfoot through the streets of Tel Aviv, chased by the girl who, I discovered afterwards, had been offered double her fee if she could catch me. But she didn't and I eventually made my way back to the hotel. I walked into my room only to find half the team waiting for me in the darkness. This time there was no escape. They held me down, pulled off my trousers and gave me a very close shave. End of initiation.

What with winning the gold medal and having had a marvellous time in Israel – I love the country which is why I chose to return there for my honeymoon in 1984 – it was scarcely possible to have a more satisfying and enjoyable introduction to the world of international tournaments. Few were to prove so easy from the contest point of view, or fascinating in other ways, but it certainly gave me a taste for the international travel which has figured so prominently ever since.

2

LONDON APPRENTICESHIP

I returned from Israel still euphoric from the victory and the whole experience. The danger of such post-competition high spirits is that they can be followed by equally devastating 'lows' as you are suddenly faced yet again with the harsh and often boring reality of a sportsman's training life, and certainly my life was about to be as uncomfortable and hard as it would ever be. From the age of 15 it had become increasingly obvious that if I wanted to progress, I would have to move to London to train with the men who were then taking British judo into the senior international competition world.

It was tempting to think that I could work from the warm, familiar and convenient family home in Leamington Spa where I was supported by my parents who encouraged me at times of tension, lifted me at times of boredom, put on the brakes if I threatened to go off the rails and shared in the successes when they came. But my father and teachers both at the Coventry Judo Club and in the Midlands area such as Brian Perryman, who has given me consistently good advice throughout my career, realised that what I really needed to develop was the environment of a level of judo that they simply could not offer in the Midlands. It was indicative of their total unselfishness and desire for my success that we began to consider the various possibilities; the sports world, as I found out later, is not short of coaches and parents desperate to hang on to their prodigies in order, it must be said, to be able to bask in the reflected glory. My father, Brian Perryman, and others at the Coventry Club were completely different. I could have continued to live in Leamington, doing my basic training, going to national squad sessions, travelling round to the competitions as most aspiring internationals living in the provinces did then and do even now. But I needed the stimulus of a different level of judo training to bring out the best in me. They realised that in Coventry, they were not sufficiently in touch with what was happening in international contest judo and they did not know the latest techniques or the advanced conditioning routines in the way that the London judo scene did.

For judo is not like running or hurdling or shot putting. It is developing and changing all the time with new throws being introduced, new, nifty groundwork moves suddenly appearing and old, forgotten techniques being rediscovered, dusted off and given new life perhaps by a slight, but cunning, change of movement. To get to the top and remain there in judo requires constant study and reappraisal and it is necessary to be at the centre of British judo, which is in London. For me, the advantages of coming to London's oldest club, the Budokwai, were partly that it was the home of many of the top competitors including Keith Remfrey, who was to win a silver medal in the 1976 Olympics, Vass Morrison, John Hindley, Dave Lawrence and also, of course, that two sessions each week were taken by the most successful and charismatic British judo competitor of the time, Brian Jacks. In addition, the Budokwai was important because it was to that long-established school just off the Fulham Road that visiting judo players from all over the country and the world would come, whether as individuals, or as a team. There were also instructors who had stopped competing such as Syd Hoare and Tony Sweeney but who had a fund of international experience on which to draw.

So, by the beginning of 1974, the question was not whether I should go down to London but when. It seemed sensible to leave school at the end of the summer term and have a short time in London before going to Israel, so it was shortly after the summer holidays that I made the break. Syd Hoare's offer of accommodation turned out to be a genuine one and I moved into a big, dark house owned by a 4th Dan named Mike Gross. I will never forget the first time I went there. The room was dark, like the rest of the house, and had been painted in different colours by the various occupants of the room before me and I found it very depressing. As a matter of pride I had accepted only two weeks' money from my parents and though they had said I should always ring them if I was having difficulty, I didn't want to do that, so I knew I had to get a job within two weeks. I sat on the bed for an hour, staring at the floor and wondering what I had done. It did not, however, take long to settle in for the house was full of judo men and I stayed there for over a year as I gradually became used to living in London. Throughout the ensuing difficulties with jobs and the constant lack of money, Mike continued to be helpful and generous, leaving me food where I would find it when I had none and being flexible on many rent days.

Of course, within hours of arriving in London, I found my way to Gilston Road, Fulham, and The Budokwai or The Society for Martial Ways. The club had a long and respected history as it was Britain's oldest judo club and had been founded in 1918 by Gunji Koizumi, dubbed in his lifetime the 'Father of British Judo', and had often employed resident Japanese instructors, brought over after consultations with the Kodokan.

The charismatic Brian Jacks winning the 1977 All-England Championships and still finding time to smile

In other words, its links with the fountain head of judo were still strong and Syd Hoare, Tony Sweeney, Charles Palmer (the last named was for many years President of the International Judo Federation and the British Judo Association and an old Budokwai hand) had all followed the traditional route to Japan, which included, in the cases of Hoare and Palmer, lessons in the Japanese language which they now speak fluently. But I confess that at 16 I was less interested or impressed by the history of the Budokwai than I was by the men who put everything they had into training on the tatami upstairs, and in particular, by one individual by the name of Brian Jacks.

I had watched Brian fight in contests and he had watched me. He used to come to every Junior nationals, and after I had won it for the third time, he gave me my first proper judo kit which was a Japanese-made jacket. As he gave it to me he said, 'When you get older, you will have to come down to London to train,' so the seed of the idea to move to London had begun as early as 13. Although I watched Dave Starbrook, Remfrey and the others, it was Jacks whom I admired the most, simply because I thought he was the best. When I look back on it, I was equally impressed by Starbrook but his personality didn't come over so strongly. Now, it is just his judo I admire. Jacks is an all-round judo man, which I love, with good tachi-waza and good groundwork. And he has always been a brilliant thinker with a fantastic, tactical brain. I have seen him go out to fight and do nothing except drop-seoi-nage just to get a decision and I have seen him go out and throw people with uchi-mata and tai-otoshi. Jacks also had the will to win, which was immense because he hated losing.

Now that we are both adults I can see we are very different. In my early days I was very arrogant but I don't think I am arrogant now. And I am pretty cool-headed for I don't go beserk in certain situations, I don't really lose my temper, and my aggression is always controlled though I think that Jacks is more hot tempered. We had our differences, but to give him his due he always said that I was going to be the best. However, I will never forget our first practice.

The first time I went to the Budokwai was on a Wednesday and I just went to watch. Jacks was running the Monday and Wednesday sessions which were the hard ones. His aim was to work you until you felt physically sick. Anyway, I looked in through the door and as soon as he saw me, he came up and said, 'I've got a surprise for you.' I had no idea what he meant until, a few days later, we practised groundwork together for the first time and he strangled me unconscious. When I came round, he was smiling and I swore on my life that I would never let him do that again. I tried to thump him, really thump him, but he was just laughing which was typical Jacks. I know now that it was only his way to get me to fight harder because that was what had happened to him in Japan, but I thought it was going too far. And if he had tried to do it again, I would probably have injured him. I have seen it happen in Japan, where first-year students are dragged off the mat because they have been strangled out by third-year students and I hate it. I think it is unnecessary. It is important to encourage young fighters but I have other ways. I have never strangled anyone unconscious, except by accident, which does happen in judo.

However, the incident did give me an inkling of what I was going to encounter at the Budokwai training sessions. I certainly didn't find them easy. I weighed 60 kilos and was often on the receiving end to begin with, partly because I had no real idea of how to get fit or prepare properly for judo. I had been practising with the seniors in Coventry since I was 13 and I had been going running with my brother since I was 15 as an adjunct to my training; we also used to do skipping and some weight training though there was little method in what we did. Gradually, I began to realise the importance of preparation though it wasn't until nearly two years later that I began to be really methodical in my fitness preparation.

Life wasn't simply one round of training sessions after another. I had to work and earn money. I found a job filling shelves and being a general dogsbody in a gift shop in Shepherd's Bush and I stayed there for nearly eight months until I was given the sack. I didn't really get the sack – they just let me go because I was taking off too much time to go training or away on trips. I had various other jobs but eventually I went to work for Terence Donovan, the photographer, who was a first Dan at the Budokwai where he trains regularly even now. I used to do all my running getting to work and back, not least because it saved on bus fares. Every evening would find me on the mat at the Budokwai. I practised with Jacks, Vass Morrison, Syd Hoare and I also used to have some really good practices with Roy Inman who has had such success since with the Women's Team. He could really throw, really devastate opponents, with his twitch for he would appear to come in for a big uchi-mata, when he hadn't moved, and would throw you with a big kosoto-gari. He was a very good judo man.

It was at this time that my tai-otoshi started to settle down, but it was also the time when I started to work on uchi-mata. When I arrived at the Budokwai, I realised that I knew nothing about preparation training and not a lot about judo either. I think my one advantage was that I wanted to learn, so I went out and asked a lot of people. I didn't confine myself to one person and gleaned what I could from many which may have been a rather selfish way of doing things but I thought it was better than having one person latch on to me. But living and training at the Budokwai undoubtedly influenced me to learn and develop an uchi-mata. Like the tai-otoshi, it was not a throw that came easily but proved to be the first major technique I learned in London, and certainly one of the most valuable and it has brought me nearly as many spectacular wins as my tai-otoshi or armlocks.

The first year at the Budokwai was very much a question of finding my feet in the adult world of judo, and as I worked on my techniques and learned to survive, I continued to enter domestic competitions with success – though it was by no means as easy as in the junior ranks. I began to work with Chris Bowles as my training partner even though he lived in Kent and therefore didn't come to the Budokwai as often as I did. But even then I realised how important it was to have a good partner with whom to do uchi-komi. He was one of those up and coming fighters like me and we met in contest a number of times; I always beat him – except on one occasion in a team match when we drew – but we became firm friends, which is typical of judo. He was twice European Junior Champion, in those early years, in 1974 and 1977, in Israel and East Germany respectively, when I also won my second Junior title. So we were always

A one-handed uchi-mata came in useful early in my career against my old rival and training partner, Chris Bowles, in the 1976 British Senior Trials

together. I remember how, when we had finished fighting in 1977, we celebrated by getting drunk together.

My first year in London was marked by two major international trips, the first being to Japan. When I was a child, I had said I was going to do this and do that, was going to win the Nationals and the World Championships . . . and that I was going to go and train in Japan. So receiving the letter from the British Judo Association which said that I had been selected to go to Japan was an ambition realised. The manager of the British team, Ray

Ross, wanted to send a senior team out there, but he also wanted to include me and he took some chances with me which I appreciate now.

We went for a month, staying in the hostel at the Kodokan. I had expected Japan to be a clean and well-ordered country and the hostel came as a bit of a surprise because it was the old Kodokan and not in a good state of repair. It was falling apart really and there were cockroaches you could have put saddles on. But at 16, you don't notice very much. In fact, you don't notice enough. Before my first practice at the Kodokan, I was really nervous. I felt that all the Japanese on the mat would be gods, but quite soon I realised that there I was on the Kodokan mat, throwing some of them and that they were not a super race after all. I was spirited and cocky and was beginning to enjoy myself when one old boy, a 9th Dan, who was standing at the side of the mat, put his stick to one side and asked me to practise.

Now there is a tradition in Japan which dictates that when you practise with one of these senior grades, you virtually throw yourself as soon as he makes an attack. It gets to the point when all the old men have to do is raise their eyebrows and you are expected to go over. But I didn't know anything about that. All I knew was that this 9th Dan had asked me for a practice and I was throwing him all over the place. I didn't hear Jacks yelling at me 'Neil, no, no, don't throw him, Oh god' and holding his head in his hands and then, when I obviously didn't hear him because I was enjoying the moment, he yelled even louder, 'Adams, stop'. Only then did I glance up and see all the 9th Dan's pupils lined up waiting for me at the side of the mat. Had they got their hands on me, they would have had a good go at tearing me apart. I am grateful to Jacks for getting me out of that one. I just didn't know what was expected of me. Of course, you rebel as a teenager, and perhaps, from our Western point of view, that kind of system seems ridiculous but we were training in their country, so we should respect their traditions.

I enjoyed my stay in Japan, though it was boiling hot, and on some days we felt as if we were being roasted alive. We would train at the Police dojo in the morning – it was an early practice, 10 a.m. to 11 a.m. – and then we would have lunch; we would always go out and have lunch somewhere. Then there would be about two to three hours' randori in the afternoon, mainly at the Kodokan where a lot of universities came to train so we had a good practice. That was more or less how we spent the month. We didn't do very much in the evening because we didn't know where to go and, in any case, we were too tired. The Police dojo was just up the road from the Kodokan but it was a horrible practice. The judoka were stiff, strong and extremely tough and it always ended up in a bit of a battle; I have never liked fighting there very much. I came across the strangling-out practice again at the dojo, and I hated it just as much then as I had done when Jacks did it to me at the Budokwai. For some reason, they made a beeline for me and used to try it on. I remember once lashing out with my fists and luckily Jacks intervened again, otherwise the man would have killed me, but I got my point over and no one tried it again. I was so determined that I was not going to be strangled out that I would have wrapped a five by two around his head. The man was obviously so much stronger and he was taking liberties. It took Jacks and somebody else to drag him off me.

On another occasion, in the same dojo, I was throwing them but I was becoming tired when about five of them lined up to take me on and were trying to throw me on the wood even though the mat was of ample size and, again, I was protected by Remfrey and Starbrook. They were really good to me. Sixteen is a bit young to go there particularly as I was plucky and refused to be pushed around. But when I went back in 1978, I felt sharper because the randori was fantastic, and though that first trip was a little too difficult for me, it was an unforgettable experience.

My second major trip abroad in 1975 was to Turku in Finland where I was to defend my European title. Although the Sovet Union is one of the leading judo nations it was the first time I had met a Russian in contest and I lost. I was a koka up from a tai-otoshi attack when I received a shido, the smallest penalty, for passivity and as in those days the penalty overruled an equal-ranking score, he went through. I felt bitterly disappointed because I had swept through the early rounds to the semi-finals and had dominated that contest. That was my first taste of defeat not through superior technique, or even on a decision but by a questionable penalty; it is a manner of defeat that has dogged my international career and I still have not become accustomed to the stale taste it leaves in your mouth. As on other occasions, I walked around the streets of Turku with a bronze medal, feeling wretched because I felt I should have been Champion.

However, I left Turku with a more light-hearted event on my mind. As in Israel, the youthfulness of our party resulted in a number of pranks including one played on Chris Bowles whom, I'm sure, will never forget it. One night, in the hotel, a number of us descended upon him, took off his clothes, pushed him out onto a flat roof which was covered in deep snow, and locked the glass door. He stood there shivering for a few moments, hoping we would relent and let him in but he quickly realised that we were simply not going to give in. Somehow, he got down though we never quite worked out how, because shinning down a freezing cold drainpipe without any clothes on needs courage as well as gymnastic ability, and made it up the back stairs of the hotel!

Although I remember still feeling that edge of disappointment when the plane touched down at Heathrow, the resilience of a 17-year-old was already urging me to look ahead. There was much to look forward to at the close of 1975, but as with most sportsmen at the time, there was just one competition that really stood out above all others – the Montreal Olympics. On paper, there was little chance of Neil Adams being on that plane to Canada, because between the idea and the reality stood the fit and capable black figure of Vass Morrison that I knew so well. As in all combat sports, domestic achievement can be measured not only by the medals and titles gained but by the people that are swept aside in the process. It is a hard fact of judo life that because of the relatively small number of top competitors, you often end up training with the very man you will have to fight. And when you sweat and learn together, some level of friendship inevitably arises.

By the time of the British Open in April 1976, I knew Vass Morrison was not only a friend but my first main senior rival who had to be overcome in order for me to advance to the number one spot in the U70k weight category. He was a cagey fighter but because he trained at the Budokwai and I had been with him to Japan, I had had ample time in which to watch and practise with him. He used to do morote-seoi-nage on the left and ippon-seoi-nage on the right. For his left seoi, he used to be able to go right down and then stand up again and he used to crucify people with that. We first met in the Trials at the close of 1975, when he won on a decision and I came fourth, and only just managed to qualify for the British Squad. The British Open was to be the second meeting. I did much better in the early rounds, though I was avoiding groundwork because the players I was fighting were all old hands, like Willie Woods, and I just couldn't afford to go down with them. So, I just relied on my throws again. Vass and I met in the final and it was a hard and merciless contest with no quarter given. At the end, he was given the decision but I could see he was breathing heavily and he had only just edged past. We walked off the mat together and he said, 'Don't you dare be disappointed with that. You are going to be unbelievable.' He was a very nice bloke.

Despite those two defeats against Vass, I nearly went to Montreal. My name was put forward by Ray Ross, the team manager, but the management committee wouldn't accept it. It was a difficult decision because Vass had beaten me twice and what is the point in holding Trials if you don't send the man who wins? But Ross argued that I would win in 1980 because I had the potential and I would also get more out of it than Vass. This was underlined when the Italian team announced that they had selected Gamba for they too were looking ahead. Now, I reckon I would

Although I was Junior European Champion, I couldn't quite edge past my Budokwai club-mate Vass Morrison in the 1976 British Open, Olympic year, but even then I was experimenting with crossgrips

have won the bronze that Vass failed to get. I would have won it because I so wanted to win it. I remember watching the fight on television at Leamington. Vass did quite well against the Japanese, losing on a koka, but when he fought the Frenchman, Patrick Vial, Vass didn't even try. I was crying with frustration and shouting at the screen, 'God, DO something.' I felt completely sick at heart. Of course, I don't know for certain whether I would have won that bronze, but I would certainly have fiercely contested it, and the experience would have been invaluable.

However, there was much to compensate in 1976 for not going to Montreal where, of course, Dave Starbrook had added a bronze to the silver he had won in 1972, and Keith Remfrey won a silver in the Open, losing to Uemura. I travelled with the British team to Sweden, France and the Soviet Union in the build-up to the Olympics, and I even made a brief sortie into another sport, wrestling.

I have tried other sports throughout my career, sometimes just to break the tedium of repetition that is an unavoidable feature of judo. I have done a little karate which doesn't really attract me, though some of the players I have seen are very good with amazingly fast feet, but I do love boxing. I have done a little bit of sparring, both in the Leamington Boys Club and with Tony Macconnell in Manchester, and you cannot appreciate the sport until you have tried it, though I think that's the same with all sports. But just try holding your hands up for three three-minute rounds; without having trained, you just can't do it. I thought I was fit and could at least last the time but my hands kept on falling down and many spar with much heavier gloves than the ones I used. It is also an extremely hard sport. I used to spar with a man who never used to hit my face but just punched my arms, and in the end, I couldn't hold them up at all. But wrestling is different because it is fairly similar to judo though there are no jacket or trousers to grab hold of. I think judo is more skilful than wrestling as

My first attempt at wrestling at the age of 17 brought me the gold medal in my weight category at the 1975 Crofton Junior Wrestling Championships when I beat the area champion in the final

certainly, there is a greater variety of techniques, but perhaps I am just biased.

On one occasion, Jacks took a few of us down to a big leisure centre somewhere, on the day of the Crofton Junior Wrestling Championships, explained the basic rules of wrestling and told us to get into the ring and fight. I took on a big guy whom I pinned in the second round and then I pinned everyone to the final which I also won. We had a lot of fun that day. I was throwing everyone for a full point in judo terms, but they were just bridging out so I was only scoring one point. To be quite honest, I could have gone into the nationals and I was tempted to try for a place in the Commonwealth Games team but I think that would have been frowned on by the wrestling association. One thing I learned from wrestling is that you have to adapt quickly. It is extraordinary how many things you can't do without a jacket, which made me realise why wrestlers are so quick to turn to leg grabs. It is about the only thing you can do that is absolutely safe. It is a very interesting experiment for judoka to take off their jackets and fight without them for once in a while.

The last judo competition of 1976, the Junior World Championships in Madrid in December, was one of the most important to date for me. It was there that I was to meet for the first time one of the best men I have ever fought and for whom I still retain an immense respect, Takushiro Nishida. He was one of the best then and he is one of the best still because he is so quick, and if your timing is slightly out, he will throw you, more often than not with kouchi-gari which is the fastest I have ever seen in my life. In Madrid I had four fights, winning three comfortably but losing, on two kokas to one, to Nishida. My groundwork wasn't good enough at this stage and I wasn't sufficiently decisive but I think the reason I really lost was that for the first time in my judo career, I felt overwhelmed. This was the first time I had fought a Japanese in contest and he just happened to be a brilliant one. The silver medal went to the man whom, even then, I didn't really consider a serious rival, Ezio Gamba. That was one occasion when we didn't meet in contest because he was on the other side of the draw.

As my judo continued to progress throughout 1976, so did other areas of my life. I was still living a hand-to-mouth existence, but it was during this year that I met two people who I was to be in daily contact with over the next four years. The first was a girl called Helen Caldwell. I had always had girlfriends, even while at school, but I am afraid that they had been placed a firm second to my judo. It was part of my selfish attitude at the time that if they weren't interested in my judo, then I wasn't interested in them. Helen was different because she did judo. In fact, we met at the Budokwai where she was practising as a capable brown belt. Just how capable she was can be seen by the fact that she is now one of the few registered stunt women and has appeared in a couple of the James Bond films. I hadn't had a girlfriend since I had come to the Budokwai, so we just started to go out together. She was older than me – I was 17 and she was 21 – and had trained as a physical education teacher, though in the end she found she wasn't really cut out to be a teacher, and is now happier doing stunt work. After a short time, she moved into my room at Mike Gross's house, and then we moved first into a room in Camberwell and next into a flat in Peckham. We stayed together for four years.

The second person was my coach, Cyril Carter. Unlike most other sports, there isn't a tradition of personal coaches in judo. Until then, very little had changed in the way judo was taught and the way competitors were trained since judo originated. It hadn't really kept up with the advanced physiological preparation that was now common practice in gymnastics and athletics and the custom for personal coaches overseeing specific training programmes was unknown. Up to the time I came down to London, my father was my personal guide. He looked after all aspects of my judo and gave me a good technical base from which to work and even the correct psychological outlook. When I came back from Israel having won my first international, everyone was saying that I would be the next Brian Jacks. But as soon as I got home, my father sat me down and said categorically: 'You are not going to be the second Brian Jacks, you are going to be the first Neil Adams.' And he meant it both psychologically and technically. He didn't want me to copy Jacks's personality or his techniques, but to develop my own. But once I had moved down to London, my father was unable to continue to influence and advise me and that role was taken over by Cyril Carter.

Cyril Carter was a former gymnast and an expert in preparation training whom I met through Jacks. Carter was helping Jacks with his conditioning and fitness and he invited me to go to Avery Hill College, where he was a physical education teacher, to do some training. He asked me what training I was doing, which was mainly judo and running, and it quickly became clear to him that I knew nothing about diet, training habits or preparation for contest. For the first time, it occurred to me that perhaps I should be doing some specific training in the pre-contest weeks, and different training during the early months of a build-up. In a way, Cyril didn't know what was required for judo so we were both learning.

The first thing he insisted on was the use of a training diary. There are three very good reasons for keeping a daily record of your training. Firstly, you are constantly learning new techniques and training methods and it is impossible to keep such knowledge at instant recall, whereas writing down everything you learn and experience gives you something to refer back to. It also helps you sort out the good practices from the bad. Secondly, when you have learnt and adopted some kind of structure schedule, the diary provides feed-back in terms of the successful and the unsuccessful elements. Lastly, a training diary can help to prevent the sportsman from becoming 'coach dependent', because it helps to provide the necessary information for the player to set out his own short-term goals and to formulate long-term aims and objectives.

I used to write down everything in my training diary. I wrote down how I felt during the day, including whether I felt mental pressure one day, and physical pressure the next. I wrote down which throws worked in randori, why and on whom, and why others didn't. I made a note of exactly what I did, how far I ran, which weights I pushed, what I didn't do and why. And I tried not to cheat.

I also described what I observed, particularly about other judo players who were in my weight or above, and through that I became accustomed to watching and analysing, instead of just going on the mat and getting up a good old sweat. And after contests, I would fill pages and pages with my reports so that I knew the strengths and weaknesses of every player I was likely to come across. Although I have never been very good at mathematics or thinking logically, I can now retrieve and use information about opponents very quickly. But at the start I had to write my thoughts down. So, for instance, about Chris Bowles, I wrote: 'Main throw, ouchi-gari (not very strong tai-otoshi). Seoi-nage under pressure. Gripping good. Doesn't like left-handers. Left-hand grip with right foot forward.' Then I would note the last time I fought him: 'Three minutes fighting for grips, attacked him with seoi-nage. Nothing. Tai-otoshi, scored koka. Ouchi-gari, scored koka. Let him attack with ouchi-gari, countered, scored waza-ari.' Or I would put in reasons why he made it difficult for me, what I did, why I changed my tactics halfway through. I made the same kind of entry for all my opponents.

The training diary and programmes set by Cyril helped me enormously and I doubt whether I would have achieved so much had I not met him. A lot of people now ask why I still keep on consulting Cyril when I can clearly run my own training now. But Cyril goes a long way back for me, and he has helped me in the past, paid for me when I had no money, and I remain grateful. While my father provided my ethics and basic judo knowledge, Cyril provided me with a framework with which I could confidently enter the senior international world of judo which was fast approaching.

Since judo is a relatively recent addition to the international sports scene – it first appeared in the Olympics in 1964, and only became a permanent fixture in the Olympic programme in 1972 – the rules of competition were still evolving at this stage. The 1964 Olympics had followed the Japanese ideal of having few weight categories: there were two, the U70k and the U93k, plus the supreme crown, the Open category. But the exigencies of modern sport forced Japanese ideals to compromise, and when judo reappeared in 1972, it was with four weight categories: U63k; U70k; U80k; U90k; and the Open. In 1977, a new system of seven weight categories and the Open was adopted as the new international standard and it has remained unchanged since then. They are: U60k; U65k; U71k; U78k; U86k; U95k; Over 95k; and the Open. As I was used to fighting U70k, the changes had little immediate effect on me though they were to be crucial later on.

By 1977, I had had a frequent taste of senior level competition, both at home and abroad, but the year started off with my first Senior British Open title which signalled to both domestic and international U71k contestants that I had finally arrived. Vass Morrison had retired from international competition after the Olympics, but returned to Crystal Palace in April for the Open, though at U78k, where he met and beat Brian Jacks. The defeat was not unexpected, for Jacks had only recently come out of hospital where he had received treatment for a dislocated back which had paralysed him for a few days. Both seemed happier at U78k, and it left me a fairly clear run in the U71s, to the final, where I met the Swede, Ronnie Nilsson, whom I had already fought on a number of occasions. It was an all-action affair, with Ronnie getting in an attack straightaway, which I avoided. A few seconds later, I scored a koka from a tai-otoshi, and Ronnie then conceded a chui penalty for stepping out of the area. I then caught him with a kouchi-gari for yuko and another tai-otoshi, scoring yuko, which closed the scorecard, and gave me a comfortable win. It was the first of eight Senior British Open titles I have won to date, and it put me in a confident mood for my next international challenge, the Senior Men's European Championships in Ludwigshafen, West Germany, in May.

When I arrived in Ludwigshafen, I was still only 18 and scheduled to meet some immensely experienced and hardened fighters, but I still possessed an unshakeable faith in myself. I saw no reason why I should not win; I wasn't aiming for a bronze or a silver or a fifth place but only for gold. And it could have happened. I threw a Dutch fighter, Brandt, in the first round with tai-otoshi in 51 seconds for ippon. I was so bubbling with confidence that I wasn't worried in the least that my second fight was against one of the greatest U71k fighters of the time, the World and Olympic Champion, Vladimir Nevzerov of the Soviet Union. I literally

The 1977 European Championships in Ludwigshafen, West Germany, brought my first encounter with the World and Olympic Champion, Vladimir Nevzerov (Soviet Union), who beat me, but only just . . .

bounded out which must have given him a terrible shock. He just thought I was a kid who would collapse under the pressure of his reputation let alone his skill, but my cocky attitude had no respect for past achievements. It may have been Nevzerov who had smashed the Japanese Champion Kuramoto in the Olympic final with a devastating tai-otoshi, but that had been the year before and Ludwigshafen, West Germany was another time, another place. He came out with quite a casual attitude and I remember thinking, 'This man believes he is going to throw me.' But he had a really hard time. We both got knock-downs, but his was scored while mine, which I still consider was a better throw, was ignored. We were both surprised, but there is no doubt that referees do tend to favour the senior fighter which I think is a left-over from the traditional Japanese view. Referees also favour Japanese, which is why if you want to beat a

Japanese, you have to put them away properly and not rely on a decision – as I was to find out later in my career.

Anyway, Nevzerov scraped through and when we met again a few days later in the European Team Championships, he knew what to expect. He beat me for a second time on a koka but again he only just managed to win and he knew he was fighting for his life. He accorded me a lot more respect that time too. I would have loved to have had another go at him, but he retired later that year. I saw him some time afterwards and he came up and acknowledged me even though he didn't speak any English. That was a great honour for me because he was one of the all-time greats.

In the Individual European Championships where we met first, Nevzerov naturally went through to win the final which enabled me to come back through the repechage. I threw the Hungarian Karoly Molnar for ippon, and then the Frenchman, Landart, for waza-ari, to get the bronze. Two Englishmen returned from Ludwigshafen with senior bronze medals in the Individual Championships, my larger Budokwai colleague, Paul Radburn, who won his bronze in the U95k category, and me.

A few months later, I was on the European medal hunt again, this time in East Berlin for the Junior Europeans. The unpredictability of judo is such that it is no foregone conclusion that if you win a Senior European medal, a Junior one will follow automatically. You can just meet the wrong person on the wrong day (and two wrongs here don't make a right – they mean a score against you) and fall flat on your face. But, thankfully, I didn't, though I had a hard time, and my success in that Championship was well-earned. I fought Christian Dyot of France first of all, and won because I scored in the last three seconds, having been down for most of the fight. I deserved that, because I had gone mad for the last part of that fight, putting in everything I had, to claw my way back.

I won the next two fights on kokas, and in the final I faced Ezio Gamba for the first time. I had known Gamba for some time and had watched him lose to Chris Bowles in Israel and to Nishida in Madrid. I was delighted to meet him in the final because I thought it would give me a quick victory. It was only when I took hold that I suddenly realised that not only was I facing a world-class judo brain, I was also facing someone who had done his homework on me. Those who haven't tried judo seldom realise how much can be transmitted through the initial change of grips; volumes of subtle, tactical information were being picked up by both of us on that mat in just a few seconds. I felt sure I could beat him using my superior strength and grips but I also realised that this contest would not be decided by ippon. His techniques, which were left morote-seoi-nage and kouchi-gari on both sides, made little impact on me but I had to be careful and wait patiently for the opportunity to put in an effective attack. In the end, it was decided by a koka score from my right tai-otoshi, and I took my second Junior European medal.

On my return, I continued with my training programme and domestic competition, winning the All-England Championships in October for the second successive year, by throwing Kirk Isichei for waza-ari in the final. I even found time to visit the West German Open two weeks later, which I won beating, among other people, the Pole Talaj. But I could no longer ignore the fact that I had to sort out my employment situation, and find a job which would fit in with my training. Although I was only 19, and the ILEA teacher's minimum age was 21, I was accepted as a teacher and started three years of travelling around the schools teaching judo. I didn't like it very much because I seemed to get only the bad eggs, the ones who didn't want to learn. I enjoy teaching advanced levels and I don't mind teaching the basics so long as people want to learn. But it gave me a good background because it taught me much about working with both children and adults.

It was in 1977 that the Press began to see me not as a young and talented but inexperienced fighter working in the shadow of Brian Jacks and Dave Starbrook, but as someone with a future, someone who was capable of picking up the crown left vacant by the retired senior figures. As a teenager, I had treasured every line about me that was put into print, but I had to learn to come to terms with the fact that judo was of minority interest to the general public, and what was seen as a major achievement in a judo magazine would merit only a couple of lines in the national papers. Recognition from a wider public had yet to come and in a way, though I wouldn't have agreed at the time, I wasn't good enough technically for the full glare of the public spotlight. Constant success in domestic competitions from the age of ten meant that I had inevitably lost some of my ability to assess myself critically and not even my candid training diary could correct that.

In short, my groundwork was way behind the standard of my standing work. It wasn't bad but it couldn't be relied on under pressure. Yet I had been so adroit at covering up the weakness, to myself as well as to everyone else, that I simply wasn't prepared for the shock when it came. But the defeat I suffered at the hands of Jean-Pierre Gilbert in the final of the 1978 British Open Championships in Crystal Palace, when he strangled me into submission with a skilful sangaku-jime, shamed me into undertaking a serious study of my judo. For too long, I had relied essentially on an abundance of natural talent, a profound desire to win and a bit of hard work. Now I had to go back to judo school. I wasn't useless on the ground. I had proved that in Japan and by winning my share of contests with hold-downs, and the occasional armlock and strangle. But though I was always a handful on the ground, I didn't have any positive tactics.

On the advice of the British team manager, Tony Macconnell (who ran the team with Dave Starbrook), I had decided to enter the British Open at 78 kilos, though my natural weight was still only 73 kilos. The idea was that harder fights with heavier opponents would sharpen me up and prepare me better for top-level competition at the European Championships in Helsinki the following month. All went well until I met Gilbert in the final.

Gilbert had done well on his side of the draw but I still did not anticipate any real problems in dealing with him. I had beaten all my early opponents in under four minutes with uchi-mata and even juji-gatame, and went into my last fight of the day with confidence. But Gilbert had been watching me carefully and managed to smother all my best standing attacks. I did manage to knock him down to the ground with a kouchi-gari but that was exactly where the Frenchman wanted me. After some manoeuvring by both of us, I suddenly found myself clamped in a leg strangle from which there was no escape and I had no choice but to submit, right in front of my home crowd. I found it the most humiliating defeat I had ever

This was the sangaku-jime strangle by Jean-Pierre Gilbert (France) in the U71k final of the 1978 British Open that forced me to completely re-examine my groundwork

experienced. I was devastated. I came off the mat not knowing where to go but Brian Perryman, from the Coventry Judo Club, came up to me, looked me right in the eyes and said: 'You needed that'. I didn't know how to take it at the time but now I know he was absolutely right. Afterwards I went out for a Chinese meal with Brian Jacks who tried to console me and told me not to worry, but I felt deeply ashamed. Within two days I was back on the mat having done some hard thinking and talking with Macconnell and we had agreed that I should start to look at other techniques instead of just throwing as I had done for so many years. I realised then that my attitude to groundwork was simply immature and I really started to knuckle down and research some different techniques. I had already begun to do a bit of juji-gatame but then I really pushed it.

Strangles were very popular at the time, but I wanted to try something different and I soon found out that many opponents were taken by surprise when I started attacking their arms rather than their necks. But I think I am also temperamentally attracted to the armlock because, like an ippon throw, it ends the contest so quickly and dramatically. I began to look at various ways into the armlock and I thought I had pinched my first from Iastkevich, the Russian U86k player who had used it so devastatingly, but when I looked again at the video of his technique I found that I had misinterpreted it. Mine was working but for different reasons. Then I began adding to that repertoire, with more ways into it, and even combining it with strangle attempts. As 1978 unfolded, I found myself spending as much time training on the ground, practising newaza uchi-komi, as I was standing. Even so, it wasn't until about a year later that I began to feel really confident on the ground and now I will take on anyone, so long as it is on my terms. The trouble is that not very many people are prepared to take me on. I have lost count of the number of times I have heard coaches yell at their charges in the middle of a contest when I have lured them into groundwork to get away and get up!

Developing my groundwork was, of course, a long-term project but in the meantime I had to go on fighting and the next contest on the cards was the European Championships in Helsinki. One of the intriguing aspects of judo is that it is rarely possible to prejudge a contest between two men who are of fairly equal standing, because while their styles may neatly dovetail into one another's giving one a slight superiority, the two styles may just as well clash and the contest can turn into a heavy brawl.

Helsinki started well for me with a victory (two kokas) over Ronnie Nilsson of Sweden, and I then went on to beat Ognian Atanasov of Bulgaria and Martin Woss of Austria; I lost to Tuma of Czechoslovakia through a penalty (I grabbed the inside of his sleeve by mistake when I tried an uchi-mata) but had amassed enough points to get out of the pool. I was then faced with the East German Gunther Kruger whom I have fought on many occasions. In this crucial match, I scored a yuko from a left ippon-seoi-nage – he just went over – so shortly afterwards I tried it again but Kruger just killed it stone dead. The matter should have ended there but the referee gave me a chui penalty for negatively dropping on my knees and as, in those days, a chui overruled a yuko, Kruger was given the decision despite the fact I had done most of the attacking. I was furious because I felt it was unjust. So I was absolutely boiling with rage by the time I came out to face Valery Dvoinikov, the extremely able Soviet fighter whom Kruger had surprisingly armlocked. I immediately scored a koka for a kouchi-gari, then a yuko for tai-otoshi. I couldn't believe it for Dvoinikov was no novice. He had won the silver medal in Montreal in 1976 after throwing everyone up to the final with a spectacular kata-guruma, and despite being short, he was known for his explosive power. Believe me, he had muscles bigger than Superman's. But there I was, whitewashing him. Finally, I took hold of him and threw him for ippon with another tai-otoshi with less than a minute to go. Macconnell just couldn't understand it because half an hour earlier Dvoinikov had been thrashing everyone else, including Kruger, until he was caught in an armlock. But there is no accounting for styles, mix and blend, but I was really made. I returned with yet another bronze.

From the point of view of competition, 1978 was proving to be one of my busiest years. Every month, it seemed, I was travelling either in Britain or to the Continent to fight. I fought and won the Swedish Open, the Polish Open (winning all my fights with ippon against opponents of such calibre as Talaj, Molnar and the rugged East German Lehmann), and the All-England for the third successive year (throwing Bill Ward for ippon with tai-otoshi). I again fought in the British Closed and produced ten ippon throws from ten contests to the final where I threw Dave Walker, again for ippon. But behind these tangible successes was the all-too familiar British story of all-too intangible money. In short, I was broke, but for the first time I began to feel it. When I first came to London, the novelty, excitement and the challenge of making my own way in the world and climbing the rungs of the competition ladder largely concealed the strain of constantly living on the breadline.

By 1978 I was 20, and despite the medals and the recognition, my standard of living had not risen because teaching judo is not the most lucrative of occupations – particularly when most of the time has to be devoted to training. I had also experienced a different lifestyle for, when you travel abroad with the British team, you stay in good hotels most of the time and eat well. You mix with the leading judo players of other nations, most of whom come from countries which don't have the same penny-pinching attitude that prevails in British sport. They are regarded as full-time athletes and they are supported as such. But each time I went abroad, I returned to the dismal reality of a lack of money. Although I had passed my driving test at the age of 17, I still didn't have enough money to buy a car, even an old banger. The wheels of financial support were in motion following my bronze medal success in Europe in May, but were taking a long time in getting to me. When I came back from Poland, I spoke for the first time in national newspaper interviews about my difficulties. Shortly afterwards, I received an offer from Arnold Humphries, of Dunn Engineering, who not only gave me a nominal post but also an old van. Shortly after that, came the first of a regular series of grants from the Sports Aid Foundation.

In addition to those two sources of help came a third, from the Winston Churchill Fellowship, specifically to allow me to go to Japan for another month's training session and to take part in the Japanese Open, the Kano Cup. The trip was completely different from my first visit at 16, first of all because it was absolutely freezing. We had been invited to stay at the home of Watanabe, who had been the senior instructor at the Budokwai for a while in the early 1960s, and it would have been discourteous to refuse such an offer. The trouble was that there was no heating at his flat and it was about 15 miles away from the Kodokan, so we had to travel back and forth all the time. There was even a three-mile walk to the station to catch the train. We had bed rolls, but it was freezing, and there was no running hot water. In the end, most of the team – which included Ray Neenan, Bill Ward, Brian Jacks and Arthur Mapp – moved back to the Kodokan hostel, leaving only Macconnell and me at the flat. Actually, we should have known it was going to be a difficult time, because to save money someone had booked us on Albanian Airlines, or something like that, and it took us 28 hours to fly to Japan, stopping off en route in just about every tinpot country which boasted a road for an airstrip and also in some that didn't even have that. We had two days to get over our jet lag before being launched into some light training in preparation for the Kano Cup and we needed every hour of it.

It was a good competition for me to end the year on but it was also important for another reason. I started well, armlocking Tambour (Belgium) and then throwing the Hungarian, Molnar, for ippon with tai-otoshi. My third fight again brought me face to face with Takushiro Nishida who had beaten me in Madrid in the 1976 Junior World Championships and was the favourite to win the U71k category. This time

I had done my homework on him, but it was obvious that he had simply forgotten me. He never made that mistake again. Shortly after we took hold, I tried my tai-otoshi but Nishida casually stepped over it. A little too casually, I thought, and I came in again as if for tai-otoshi but switched to uchi-mata at the last moment. Nishida was caught completely straddled on my leg, and he went clean over the top for ippon. For a moment, the packed crowd in the Nippon Budokan Hall in Kudanshita, Tokyo was shocked into silence until the European contingent burst into ecstatic applause. It was a sweet moment. And, after that, I couldn't wait to go on for the next fight against another Japanese, Yoshimura. Unfortunately it was rather an anti-climax, a tense battle for grips in which he was given the decision, and he went on to win the competition, leaving me with a bronze. But that throw on Nishida was worth it.

I have met Nishida since and we have marvellous practices. There is a strength difference now because he still weighs around 71 kilos, but I have to be on guard because he remains so incredibly fast. I would rate him as one of the best judo players I have ever practised with and he inspires some of my best judo. You just don't know whether he is going to attack with kouchi-gari, right drop seoi-nage, or left sode-tsuri-komi-goshi as he has a never-ending stream of inventions. Jacks won a bronze in that competition as well for he was held down by Takahashi but it was a good result for him because he was coming back after a long lay-off. It was also his last competition, so it was good to end on a positive note.

The uchi-mata with which I threw Nishida effectively established me in Japan. Apart from France and, of course, Britain, I am best known in Japan now and I am always extremely well treated when I go there; I have been to Japan only once since and I would like to go again. The Japanese have so much depth in the top calibre that they could probably produce a dozen like Yoshimura, though they do struggle in certain weights such as the Under 86s and Under 95s. The Japanese 'feel' different from Westerners; I could be put blindfold on to a mat and just by taking grip I would know whether I was on with a Japanese because of their technical fluency. I have also found them a very humble people – off the mat.

We stayed out there until Christmas and expected to fly home in time for the holiday period but the weather closed in and the flight home was nearly cancelled. Ray Neenan started to talk mournfully about the possibilities of putting Christmas decorations up in Watanabe's freezing flat, but luckily, we made it back. I am an Englishman through and through and however much I love judo, Christmas is not to be spent sitting huddled on a futon in a freezing flat 15 miles outside Tokyo, but by the warmth of an English hearth.

3

MY FIRST OLYMPICS

The ideal of judo for all Japanese is for the small man to despatch the larger man through a combination of skill, speed and spirit. It is not purely to do with the high regard the Japanese have for small things which work as well as large things – from miniature televisions to tiny calculators – because in the world of Japanese sport, the Sumo wrestler looms large at 160 kilos and above. It is because, in Japanese terms, it means that the principle underlying judo, the famous 'maximum efficiency through minimum effort', which was set out by Jigoro Kano, is demonstrated perfectly when a lightweight catapults a heavyweight through the air. That is why the most popular competition in Japan has always been the All-Japan Championships which have no weight categories.

However, in practice, it is generally only possible for the small to overcome the large when there is a considerable disparity in technical ability, and one indisputable fact about judo is that the technical standard of players all over the world has improved enormously over the past 15 or 20 years since it became an Olympic sport. Despite the fact that the Open category is traditionally the senior crown of judo, it is increasingly becoming just a second heavyweight competition which is one reason why it is likely to be axed from the 1988 Olympics in South Korea. In recent years, a few light-heavyweights have entered the Open categories of the major championships but very few, and notably only the Belgian World Champion Robert Van de Walle, have fought with any distinction. In fact, as the technical standard of the international competitors rises, and the difference between the top players becomes more one of style than of standard, weight categories are becoming increasingly important. There are always the occasions where exceptions occur such as the epic battles in the past few years between two former World Champions, the Anglo-French heavyweight Angelo Parisi and the light-heavyweight Van de Walle, in which the honours have been fairly even despite the disparity in weight. However, such contests are savoured all the more because they are so rare.

It is against this background that the problems of weight control must be seen. At least three-quarters of contestants in any major cham-

The incomparable Angelo Parisi, a former Budokwai member, throwing Olympic Champion Shota Chochosvili for ippon after the Russian had been leading the open weight category semi-final in the 1977 European Championships, West Germany, by a waza-ari and two kokas. This is judo!

pionships will have had to lose two, three or even more kilos from their training weight to 'dip' under on the scales the night before or sometimes on the morning of the contest. This is not because the loss of a few pounds will make much difference to their performance, necessarily, but because each weight category employs a different fighting style. The heavyweights cannot hope to match the speed and athleticism of the lightweights whereas the lightweights cannot match the 'propping' ability of the heavyweights. In its way, for me to fight against heavyweights would be as exceptional as for Steve Ovett suddenly to enter the 10,000 metres or marathon. A false impression is given in judo by the daily training sessions in which the large and small, the young and old, the advanced and the beginners all seem to mix together without harm. And it is great fun. I have practised with all the 'big boys' in Britain, including Paul Radburn and Elvis Gordon, our heavyweight and open representatives in the Los Angeles Olympics, as I have practised with our lightweights, Neil Eckersley and Stephen Gawthorpe. I have also had some good sessions with Van de Walle at a couple of training camps in Paris and he is a strong fighter. But in the same way as runners have carefully to consider the distance which suits them best in conjunction with the practicalities of existing opponents, so the adult judo player has to consider his optimum weight which is partly dictated by natural factors and partly discovered by trial and error. I sometimes think that my fighting career in this sense has been punctuated by more errors than trials. Even in late 1977, the question was raised whether I should go up to 78 kilos or continue to come down from about 73 or 74 kilos to U71k. It is always tempting to decide to come down a weight rather than to go up because the strength factor should be to your advantage unless you have starved yourself so much to make the weight that you are too weak to take on a row of children, let alone one of hardened men.

By the beginning of 1979, the approach of the Olympics, not to mention the World Championships in Paris at the end of the year, made the question of weight category a crucial one and it remained a constant shadow throughout the year and half of the next. I started the year by going down in weight, fighting the 1979 British Open at U71k, though I had felt sufficiently confident the year before to fight at U78k until I had met Gilbert in the final. Despite having recently been laid low by a virus infection, I had little trouble throughout the day, overcoming various domestic opposition (including Peter Blewett, who now teaches at the Budokwai) before meeting the Swiss Eric Lehmann in the final. Though fast and fit, he fell prey to my kouchi-gari and tai-otoshi before I caught him on the ground and held him with kesa-gatame. It gave me a certain amount of personal satisfaction that I won the title on the ground after having lost it through groundwork the previous year. It demonstrated, I hoped, that I had improved.

My weight shot up again to 74 kilos after the Open but I lost it weeks later for the National Team Championships in Glasgow in May where I armlocked my old friend from the Midlands, Bruce Newcombe, in the final. With the European Championships in Brussels at the end of the month, I couldn't afford to let my weight go back to normal and I spent the rest of the time dieting. My weight was just about manageable, if I was careful, but it was becoming more and more of a problem.

Cyril Carter advised me to make the transition to U78k during the 1979 season but he was teaching and coaching in the United States at the time, and was unable to influence me. He was not alone in his view for Tony Macconnell who, with Dave Starbrook, managed the British team from 1976 to 1980, also tried to persuade me to go up. Macconnell has been one of the most prominent figures in British judo – though he has also spent some time abroad, coaching the Swedish team among others – and then, as now, I respected and liked him. Lancashire-born, he is one of the most amusing men I know, and at the same time, an enthusiast whose great skill is in inspiring judoka both in training and as a mat-side coach. We knew each other well and I listened to him, but psychologically and even physically, I felt that once I made the weight I was perfect at U71k and was extremely reluctant even to consider fighting in the higher weight category at the Olympics.

So, back I went down the scales for the 1979 European Championships in Brussels. With two bronze medals at previous Senior European Championships, I had one purpose only in going to Belgium and this time I didn't make a mistake. I threw Ronnie Nilsson in nine seconds, a Hungarian called Nagysolymosi in eight seconds and a Belgian within a minute. I gained my revenge for the previous year's loss against Kruger by throwing him with tai-otoshi in the opening seconds for yuko and dealt similarly with Christian Dyot of France. This placed me against Ezio Gamba again and it turned out to be a repeat of the 1977 Junior European Championships. When we took hold, it was clear that this was a different Gamba again for he was stronger, faster and more experienced. But nothing could dent the overwhelming confidence which I felt and in a way I didn't really question the outcome. I caught him with a tai-otoshi for a koka and collected my first Senior European title.

I came home triumphant, of course, because there I was, at 20, seemingly on course for the World and Olympic titles that I had coveted for so long. But I remember telling David Hunn of the *Observer*: 'Everybody needs luck in judo, and if I'm lucky and if I can put it together on the day, I know I can do it, I know that.' Even with a European title in my pocket, a certain caution, for I don't remember mentioning the word 'luck' before in an interview. Perhaps I was getting older or (and more likely) I was beginning to feel the public pressure of being expected to win.

Unlike the build-up to the Los Angeles Olympics in 1984, I had freedom to train as well as relatively few financial or emotional worries,

The aggressive and experienced East German Gunther Kruger had to be beaten in Brussels in 1979 en route to my first Senior European title, but on that day nothing could stand in my way

---

with the support from the engineering company continuing, and my life with Helen Caldwell being relatively comfortable though the relationship was beginning to show signs of strain. But suddenly, I began to realise that it is easier to be the unknown underdog, fighting for recognition, than 'one of Britain's Olympic medal prospects'. As the Moscow Olympics grew nearer, I became the focus of more Press attention than ever before, with appearances on *Blue Peter* and articles in women's magazines, as well as on the sports' pages.

That European Championship highlighted an aspect of judo which is far from the friendly club world but part and parcel of top-level international competition – playing the rules. The previous year I had had a special jacket made which was designed to fit me exactly and yet stay within the rules. Most judo techniques depend on the fighters being able to grip each other's jacket and trousers and if it is difficult to get a good grip, it can prove much more difficult to throw effectively. My jacket was legal but only just. Now some people may feel that such gamesmanship represents the unacceptable face of sport but I disagree. The rules are there to set limits and I wasn't breaking them or even bending them. I was just taking them to the limits which is what happens in other areas of competition as, for instance, when you play an opponent tactically which, in itself, is part of the ethos of judo, I believe, rather than any woolly sense of English fair play. Anyway, when we came off the mat Kruger complained that my kit was too tight and he couldn't get a grip. I had packed my kit away and was asked to take it out and allow it to be checked and, though it was obviously near the mark, there was nothing illegal about it. In fact, I have never had to change jackets though I have spotted illegal ones on others, and requested that they should be changed. But I do go to quite a lot of trouble to check out the opinions of many different referees when a new rule is introduced. I regard that as part of a professional attitude towards the sport rather than simply a way to 'cheat' legally.

The final competition of the year was the December World Championships in Paris, the first time for four years the competition (normally biennial) was taking place. The 1977 competition had been cancelled by Charles Palmer, then President of the International Judo Federation, in order to forestall the event being used for political propaganda in the way the Olympics suffered so badly. I looked forward to it with confidence after my performance in Brussels, but it was coming at the end of a busy competitive year for me. So the last thing I needed when I arrived at the Pierre de Coubertin Stadium in Paris, where I have fought on so many subsequent occasions, was a hard draw but luck was not with me this time. So much can depend on a draw. A light draw can place you feeling fresh in a final while a hard draw can give you your toughest opponent in the first two fights. I generally like a couple of easy fights to give me time to warm up but that is rarely possible in the World Championships which is generally a more difficult event than the Olympics despite the great public interest the latter attracts. This is because the World Championships consists of the stronger judo nations while the Olympics draws others who decide to have a go. I wasn't under any illusions about my first senior World Championships, particularly when I saw the draw; if I had won Britain's first world judo title then I would have earned it. It would have been a satisfying moment too because for the first time, my parents had travelled abroad to watch me fight and so had my friend and former employer, the photographer Terence Donovan.

I met the experienced Pole, Marian Talaj, in the first fight and beat him on decision after a gritty contest. It was followed by a somewhat easier victory over the Yugoslav, Vujevic, whom I threw, and a sudden dominance over my old rival, Kruger, whom I caught on the ground and armlocked. Even now I can't believe the ease with which that arm came out. And again I was confronted with Ezio Gamba. Once past him, I would face the Japanese Katsuki in the final. But I never made it. From the start I felt my normal confidence against him. I knew he was strong and fast but I had never regarded him a real threat and for the first four and a half minutes, I couldn't have been more in command. I felt a subtle change of tactics in the Italian, but I felt I was handling him comfortably, until he ripped into me with a spectacularly fast left morote-seoi-nage and I was so casual I just couldn't escape from it. He scored a yuko and I couldn't equal it. I was annoyed with myself because I had felt that the world title was going to be mine and I had failed to achieve it. I was convinced that I was capable of facing and beating the best the world could put forward – in this case, Katsuki, who went on to beat Gamba – but I lost the chance to prove it. And I could blame no one but myself. I had little difficulty with Christian Dyot of France to win a bronze medal, but it was merely a question of retrieving a fragment of lost honour – my heart wasn't in it.

I spent the Christmas of 1979 at home with my family in Leamington but, though I enjoyed it, it was still something of an ordeal. I could look back over the year and see that I was well on the road to the Olympics, but that was more or less all I could do: the weight factor was so crucial, I could do little else – and I certainly couldn't eat. My constant thought was: 'If I eat that, it's a kilo' or 'I could lose half a kilo if I ran there.' My diet had gone from eating literally rabbit food to missing meals entirely and the empty feeling in my stomach meant that I was probably weighing around 71 kilos. On top of this, I was attempting to follow a full training programme which involved rigorous preparation training during the day followed by a tough judo practice during the evening. When I returned to London in the New Year, training became very tough as Olympic year brings long-forgotten judo men out of the woodwork all hoping against hope for a chance of a place in the team. It was even worse because, at 21, I tended to overtrain and become obsessional about it. I did weight training and running and if I wanted to go for a second run, I would. I was out seven days a week, at all times of the day and night, and training secretly after Macconnell or Starbrook had told me that because I had a cold, I should rest. I know better today than to train through illness but when you still feel you are serving your apprenticeship, nothing will stop you.

Without the necessary nourishment required to sustain such a pace, my body's resources inevitably became run down. So much so that it resulted in horrific mouth ulcers and glandular problems. It became so bad that, at one time, I had more than 30 ulcers in my mouth and down my throat and my lips and cheeks swelled up to almost three times their normal size. In February, I was given tests in Camberwell Hospital and they diagnosed it as a 'glandular problem' and, of course, I was ordered to rest. But by this time I was well into my build-up for the British Championships, and it would have been impossible to abandon training completely. I continued to train gently and resigned myself to slowing down my build-up and it was at this time that it was decided I should fight in the British Open at 78 kilos and possibly do the same for the European Championships in Vienna the following May. In retrospect, this should have been a positive move to abandon the lower weight category entirely. However, I still believed enough in the lower weight to consider dropping back down to 71 kilos for the Moscow Olympics in July, partly because having won a bronze medal in the World Championships I would be seeded at that weight.

Now, with the benefit of hindsight, that decision seems crazy to me. If my only chance of going to the Olympic Games had been at U71k, then it may have been a wise move to come down (as many other players are forced to do) but that wasn't the case for me. I was the best at both weights in Britain and, it seemed, in Europe as the next few months were to prove. Adapting to a change in weights is not simply learning to deal with opponents of greater power. Minor, but important, alterations have to be made to your techniques to compensate for the difference in the height and balance of your opponents. You can hit an U78k player with the same kind of technique that you use against an U71k player, except that you have a bit more weight to add yourself, but it may not work because of the slight change in the height/weight/balance factor and what would have been an ippon becomes a yuko; what would have been a yuko doesn't move the man at all. At first it seems that you are slightly below par, as if you have been ill and have lost your edge. But it is more than that. Technically, you need to rethink and readjust and as the techniques have to be used at top speed, beyond conscious control, they need to be deeply ingrained until they become almost second nature. It took me two years before it really 'clicked'. But I had had an indication the previous year that the higher weight was the correct one when Macconnell and I had decided to experiment with my first competition abroad at 78 kilos, the Hungary Cup. I not only won, but won against the current European Champion, the East German Harald Heinke, who was an extremely powerful and muscular judo man, standing about six feet tall.

My first two competitions at the higher weight in 1980 underlined the fact that 78 kilos was my optimum weight. I won the British Championships relatively easily even though I hadn't really adjusted to the differences in weight and height. My training also went well for the European Championships in Vienna. From about 1978 I had started doing my conditioning training with an amateur wrestler called Jan Curtis, who was to become a very close friend of mine, and eventually was best man at my wedding. I had met him at the Budokwai the year before when I was 19. He was actually wearing a white belt and was beating quite a few of the brown belts and first Dan black belts around. So when I came into the club, I was sent over to him. We had a good practice and I think he was quite surprised because though I looked rather young, I was causing him some problems, and he asked: 'Who the hell are you?' I told him and we started talking and went for a drink afterwards and that was the start of a special kind of friendship. He trained with me every day soon after that – running, weight training and circuits. But I didn't have a judo partner at the time and it wasn't until as late as 1982 that I realised that I needed one. While preparing for the Moscow Olympics, I just did my judo training in the evenings at the club.

When I arrived in Vienna for the European Championships, I felt under less pressure than I had done for a long time. With the Olympics still at the forefront of my mind, I was only around 74 kilos and really intent on doing the best I could but without expecting too much though, typically, I did expect to win a medal. It was clear from the start that I was far too light for the weight category, and my throws were completely 'off', but all that groundwork I had done in the post-Gilbert era now paid dividends. In the final, I faced Heinke again. Heinke had been European Champion at this weight in 1978 and 1979 and was hoping to complete the hat trick. He had caught me in the preliminaries with his strong ouchi-gari scoring a koka but I had amassed sufficient points to come through. (Incidentally, that was the last time a score, other than a penalty or a decision, was given against me until 1984.) He went into the final confident that he would repeat his earlier success and unaware that I had decided on a complete change of plan. My standing throws to the front were not working well, but my kouchi-gari was, and my groundwork was far superior to his. Early on in the fight, we went to the ground and I clung to his back like a limpet and refused to let go. I forget the number of times I nearly had his arm in the match, and if I had had the power then that I have now, I would have armlocked him with ease. Almost the entire contest was fought on the ground, with Heinke trying to avoid submitting; twice I had him in my rolling juji-gatame, and each time his superior strength prevented me from straightening out the arm and finishing the job. Nevertheless, I won the match easily on an unanimous decision and became Senior European Champion for the second time, but this time, at 78 kilos.

And so, to the final period of my preparation for the Olympic Games which had really been my single goal of the past four years. I am still not sure why the Olympics are so special when you basically fight the same people as you do in a World Championship. But there is a quality about them, an atmosphere generated by the eyes of the world, which makes even the tension different. After the European Championships, my confidence was extremely high but I was dieting again with a vengeance. It was decided that we should spend a month at a training camp in France immediately before the Games, but this turned out to be a disastrous mistake. Normally, at that time of the year, that particular training camp would provide the perfect opposition against which to train; each day would be spent doing conditioning training, but there would be 90 minutes or so of quality judo against opponents from all over the world. Indeed, the first day of every week at the camp provided some incredibly stiff opposition, but these were 'holiday' judoka, and one day practising with a British team training for the Olympics was enough for them. It resulted in the whole team ending up by training against each other for four days of the week and this was supplemented by an increase in the amount of preparation training and conditioning off the mat. The boys were also starting to bicker and fall out with each other due to the intensity of the training combined with the frustration of being without different randori partners and the fact that we had already been together for the two months leading up to this training camp; everyone ended up becoming sick of the sight of each other, and all we wanted to do was get the Games over – which was not the best of psychological approaches.

It was mid-July when the team boarded the plane for Moscow. It was a relatively young group in comparison with the one that went to the Montreal Olympics, but there were still hopes of emulating if not improving on the silver and two bronzes gained in 1972 by Remfry, Parisi and Starbrook; such is the confidence of youth. Everyone in the team knew each other well: John Holliday (U60k); Ray Neenan (U65k); me at U71k; Chris Bowles (U78k); Peter Donnelley (U86k); Mark Chittenden (U95k); Paul Radburn (O95k); and Arthur Mapp in the Open and so the general optimism was not misplaced. For Donnelley had been fighting consistently well through the year and Chris had won a silver medal in the European Championships in Vienna. However, the sky over Moscow was not without its clouds. The political arguments that were still taking place had clouded these Games as profoundly as they were to do the 1984 Games in Los Angeles except that judo was especially undermined by the absence of the Japanese. Like many British sportsmen, I had spoken publicly against the boycott: 'We all believe that politicians shouldn't play

Judo – the gentle way? A predominance of muscles when the British team for the Moscow Olympics bared its top half, left to right: Paul Radburn (heavyweight); Mark Chittenden (light heavyweight); Peter Donnelley (middleweight); Chris Bowles (light middleweight); Arthur Mapp (Open); me (lightweight); Ray Neenan (featherweight); and John Holliday (bantam weight)

---

around with sport in this way,' I had said in one article. I continued: 'There are men in the squad who have given up their jobs and worked for years for the chance to go, and I think we would walk to Moscow if we had to.' And I meant it.

Despite the political controversy, we were not looking forward to a month in Moscow for those of us who had been there before didn't have a very high opinion of the country or its hospitality, even though we expected our stay to be better than normal because we would be in the Olympic village. And it was better, though it was still typically 'Russian'. The security around the camp was unbelievable, the food made everyone ill and the only special entertainments were Russian ones. To cap it all, I still weighed 73 kilos which meant that for the following two and a half weeks, I would have to train and diet. My weight was constantly on my mind and it was bad for my morale when the rest of the boys went for meals while I stayed in the apartment.

The judo men I was to fight were scattered all over the village and instead of bumping into them all the time, which is normal at any other Championships, I saw only the occasional one at odd times. However, as is always the case in such important events, I did see Gamba all the time. We both realised that, with the Japanese not being present, we were now the favourites for the title. Incidentally, due to the political situation in Afghanistan, the Italians could send only one judo player to these Games, the rest being in the Italian Army, and it had to be Gamba. Gamba was a civilian while the other judoka in the army had to go along with the Italian Government's veto on the Games. However, having beaten Gamba in every final that I had ever fought in, I was confident that, should we meet, I would win.

During the week of the competition I was both tired and hungry. My liquid intake was also severely reduced which meant I was perpetually hungry and thirsty. The days immediately before the competition were the worst because I couldn't cheat my diet and I still had to continue training in some way almost to the time of the weigh-in. The day before, I weighed 72.5 kilos and I was in desperate need of nourishment. My friends in the team nicknamed me 'The Screaming Skull' which I thought was funny only after the weigh-in when I could eat and drink again. I trained the weight off, and was bang on 71 kilos that evening. Unfortunately, I 'cracked' during the night and had a drop of liquid, thinking that I would be lighter in the morning. I woke up to read the scales measuring 71.1 kilos and it took 15 minutes of solid skipping to take off that miserable 100 grams. After the weigh-in, I had intended to go crazy. I had had raving nightmares of bacon sandwiches, steaks, chips and gallons of fizzy, refreshing liquid. But these dreams could not, of course, be realised, because my constant dieting had caused my stomach to shrink and in that condition I could scarcely begin to do justice to my appetite.

An hour before the competition I suppose my weight must have been around 73 kilos, and I started to reflect on the draw. It was a favourable draw, with Gamba and a good Mongolian on one side, and me on the other. My first fight was against Picken of Australia. Although I had watched him train at the Budokwai in London, and knew I could beat him, I realised he was an awkward character. His judo jacket was definitely 'small' and it took me a minute to settle down. I scored a koka first with kouchi-gari, and promptly jumped on top of his back to perform the juji-gatame roll. I felt fast and in control and it seemed inevitable that he should submit and immediately his arm came out. My second fight was due to be against a Nigerian or Algerian but he didn't appear so I was given a bye to the next round.

I then faced Alksnin of Poland who was originally a U65k player, and a good one too. I knew he executed a fair seoi-nage and so I set out to dominate his grip and kill that from the start: at one point I halted an attack so strongly that I almost broke his back. I caught him with uchi-mata for a waza-ari and, unusually for me, I followed straight down with a kesa-gatame to achieve waza-ari/awazeti/ippon, the cumulative score, and my place in the semi-finals was secure.

Lehmann of East Germany was my semi-final opponent, a predominantly left-handed player, and one of the most consistent competitors in Europe. I knew that this fight could be hard and so I had told myself to go all out from the beginning. He has a very strong left tai-otoshi and this was the attack I was prepared to stop but it didn't even get that far. I attacked instantly with my right tai-otoshi and, to my amazement, the referee awarded me a koka. I think that was over-generous in the extreme – Lehmann didn't even land on his knees, he just spun around on his face, but while I have suffered from referees' curious decisions during my career, I have benefited from them as well, and this was one of those occasions. When he regained his feet, I attacked immediately with kouchi-gari, scoring another koka, and pounced on his back for the juji-gatame roll. I was surprised to find that he rolled over without difficulty and was submitting within seconds. It was a fairy tale entry into the U71k final of the Olympic Games, for I had spent little over five minutes in total on the mat. I also realised that Gamba had had a much harder time in getting to the final, and I was convinced that he would be dispensed with as easily too.

I came off the mat after fighting Lehmann feeling full of confidence and genuinely looking forward to my final against Gamba. No sooner had I stepped off the mat than I was told there was to be a five-hour break before the finals commenced and that we would be driven back to the Olympic village to eat and rest. I couldn't believe it. Here was I geared up for the most important fight of my life and, for whatever reasons, they wanted us to 'relax' for five hours. It was at this point that my immaturity and inexperience began to show. I returned to the Olympic Village almost feeling that I had already won the Olympic title and it wasn't until about three hours later that it began to dawn on me that I had yet to fight Gamba in the final and I began to feel nervous.

We made our way to the bus so that we would arrive at the warm-up area about one hour before the match was due to start. I remember the loneliness I felt sitting in the huge dojo with only Gamba for company. They started the fights for the bronze medal positions and I could hear the response of the crowd as I tried, as far as my nerves would allow me, to warm up. Dyot versus Davaadali, the Mongolian, was the last fight before mine and I was down by the side of the mat while this was going on. My stomach was churning but I was still sure that I was going to win; there was no way I would lose to Gamba in an Olympic final.

Having met Gamba a number of times, I knew what he felt like and the way he fought. He would take a secure and positive grip, move around looking for the opening and occasionally mutter aloud, though I had no idea what he way saying, because I don't speak Italian. It would probably be a bit unprintable anyway because he has a slightly crazy personality. But as soon as I took hold this time, I knew that something wasn't quite right. Tony Macconnell was on the side of the mat screaming at me to wake myself up but I was completely unsettled for the whole seven minutes. It was as if I was sleepwalking and if you don't wake up, in a seven-minute final, it can just slip away from you. I knew what I wanted to do but I found it all so difficult. My kouchi-gari, ouchi-gari, tai-otoshi and uchi-mata were all uncoordinated and I felt sluggish and uninspired. Once again, I was finding a left-hander difficult to fight. I don't even think he expected to win and I know he would have crumbled if I had scored first. But I didn't and I was rattled. At four minutes into the contest, my body was drained and I was clinging on by the skin of my teeth. At six minutes, I remember thinking, 'I've blown it'. When the bell rang it was everything I could do to drag myself to the middle of the mat for the decision but I still felt I was in with a chance. Hantei, the flags went up, two reds for Gamba. I had lost, and he was Olympic Champion.

Victory and defeat: the European Championships' 1979 Final in Brussels brought a gesture of victory from me while the Italian Ezio Gamba crumpled up in defeat. But a year later, in the Moscow Olympics, the picture was reversed

I remember standing there on the mat as the Italians were going wild; the Russians were totally unmoved because it had been such a boring contest to watch. It was probably the loneliest moment of my entire life. I didn't know what to do, I just felt sick. I also remember thinking, 'They've made a mistake. They are going to reverse the decision any moment' but of course it never happened. I stood on the mat watching the commotion that surrounded Gamba, completely numbed and lost for words. When I eventually managed to move off the mat area, my spirits at their lowest, the first thing that happened was a television reporter thrusting a microphone in front of me and saying, 'How do you feel, it was a close match?' As I was still very young and inexperienced at coping with defeat, I almost hit him but I managed to control myself and said that all I knew was I must have been one of the most disappointed sportsmen there had ever been.

One of the most fantastic feelings after winning an event like the World or European Championships is being the second to walk out to the medal ceremony because if you walk out second, of course, it means you are the winner. The first one to lead out the procession always goes to the number two spot and so on back down the line. I remember them putting me at the head of this line and as I walked out into the stadium in front of Gamba I felt absolutely sick. I was young and couldn't really handle it, especially never having been in a final of this stature before. When Gamba actually climbed onto the rostrum I remember thinking that I had never seen him on the number one spot before and why of all times did I have to see him there now. All I wanted to do, of course, was pull him down and climb up there myself! Still, I carried it off, not well, but I got through it. I would feel slightly different now.

The press conference that followed was a terrible ordeal. Trying to answer questions such as, 'How do you feel', 'Why do you think it went wrong for you?' and 'Now you have had five matches and Gamba's won one more than you . . .' was the worst feeling ever. I am a winner by nature and I find losing absolutely abhorrent especially when I know I have lost to someone whom I can beat. To me, the silver medal was in a way failing because a silver medal isn't good enough for me and also I knew that I was the better judo player of the two and hadn't performed anywhere near my best in the final. I think the first thing that hit me was that I would have to live with being the Olympic silver medallist, and not the Olympic champion. I wasn't looking forward to that at all. And it was not simply a case of possessing too large an ego.

Medals in judo are different from medals in athletics or swimming. There are only two medals in judo that can be won which are the bronze and gold. To be awarded a silver medal in judo you must have lost the last fight and therefore 'lost the gold' which is why the gold medallist, and even the bronze medallist, receive so much more acclaim. Both the gold and bronze medallists are remembered for 'winning' their medals while both the public and the competitor himself have a tendency to view the silver medal as just 'second best'. This can be seen by the simple fact that people greet the bronze medallist with 'well done' while the silver medallist receives the response 'hard luck'. Now, this may seem trivial enough, but it is a point worth realising by the competitor and might explain the depth of depression often felt by fighters who find themselves in the second slot.

What did I do that night? What could I do? I went back to the Olympic village not really aware of who or where I was. I just felt numb and put myself in the hands of Tony Macconnell. There are few people with whom I would rather have spent the aftermath of that event. He took me into a little room with a table and two chairs in it and slapped a full bottle of whisky on the table. We didn't say a word to each other. We just started on the bottle and methodically worked our way through it until we were completely paralytic. Actually, it doesn't take much to get drunk after a contest because you are so dehydrated. But we didn't just get drunk; we continued until we were literally lying on the floor with the bottle left standing empty on the table.

We got up the next morning feeling jaded to say the least but Macconnell dragged me off to the video room and sat me down in front of it. 'Right,' he said, 'now you watch the fight again and again until you decide whether you can get it out of your system and carry on, or whether you are going to give it up now.' I can't remember how many times I watched the final but Macconnell was right, it was the therapy I needed. The repetition enabled me for the first time to come to terms with the bitter feeling that I had lost. I got up from that seat prepared to face the world, and knowing that I was going to carry on.

We returned from Moscow a very disappointed team. I had won a silver and Arthur Mapp a bronze in the Open category with a fine footsweep but we didn't feel we had come up to expectations. Ray Neenan, for instance, was depressed with the way our luck had gone as he had worked extremely hard for months before the competition and was now going home without any recognition while Arthur, who hadn't trained nearly so hard and had been entered at the last minute only, was returning with a coveted Olympic medal. We also had had to wait around in Moscow for a while with nothing to do, because though we had had a bit of a party afterwards, the officials had closed the disco because all the competitors who had finished their events were getting drunk. So we were all glad to get home.

4

WORLD CHAMPION AT LAST

I thought that I had come to terms with the frustration of the Olympic gold medal slipping from my grasp in that video room in Moscow but when I returned to London, I was like a wounded animal; all I wanted was to be left alone. Everyone was, of course, very kind and understanding and I discovered for the first time the havoc I had caused in judo families up and down the country for, apparently, failure to win the gold had resulted in bad moods, people storming out of the house and getting drunk as well as a general feeling of disappointment. The thing that sickened me most was listening to television commentators saying, 'Well, that was another brave attempt by an Englishman . . .': it was all too much for me to bear.

My return prompted a major change in my living arrangements though it probably would have happened anyway, albeit not in such dramatic circumstances and perhaps with less pain to Helen, whom I left very abruptly. Helen was older than me and had been talking about getting married for some time but, at 20, I certainly wasn't ready to settle down. In fact, I was ready to move on but I shouldn't have done it the way I did; I just walked out and I know it hurt her a great deal. She didn't speak to me for some years after that though we are good friends now.

In those weeks immediately following the Olympics, I went to ground, seeing my family and a few friends but not getting back to serious training and rarely going near a judo mat. In my blackest moments, I even considered giving up judo altogether. But the sport proved to be in my blood and I felt that I still hadn't reached my peak so gradually I allowed myself to be spurred on by the two Cyrils in my life. But in order to regain my motivation, it became obvious that two things were necessary: firstly and most difficult, I had to learn from my experiences in the Moscow Olympics and secondly, I had to find some kind of short-term goal on which to focus my attention.

In forcing myself to reflect on Moscow, I first had to consider my problems of weight control and management in order to rationalise my decision to move up to 78 kilos permanently. It was going to be relatively easy to put on the necessary four or five kilos in weight but gains in body weight have to be matched by a suitable increase in strength in order to preserve the weight/strength ratio which is so vital to efficient performance. The heart and lungs must also learn to cope with the increased demands for oxygen from the now larger skeletal muscles (a process which takes considerably longer than it does to gain weight) and the player must adjust both mechanically and psychologically to his own movements as well as to those of his opponents. On top of all this, of course, I had to identify and examine the players I was likely to encounter in this new category which I had just toyed with up to now, though with surprising success.

I started training in October with the USA Open in November as my short-term goal. I went naturally up to 77 kilos – which shows how much I had been forcing my weight down – and started using slightly heavier weights. But I was still very unfit when I arrived in San José. My first fight was against Brett Barron, the American number one. I didn't know him at the time, and after a very scrappy match, I was given the decision. My next fight was against a Japanese (one of two in the competition) whom I beat by a koka and then I had another struggle against a second American whom I finally caught on the ground. That placed me in the final against Jiro Kase, the leading Japanese U78k player of the time. Of course I had no idea that we were destined to meet nine months later in the final of the World Championships in Maastricht, Holland; all I knew was that it proved to be one of the easiest fights in that tournament. As soon as I took hold of him, I threw him with tai-otoshi for waza-ari and then caught him early with the armlock move from between the legs that was to prove equally effective in Maastricht the following year. However, he fought me like mad but was unable to retrieve the waza-ari and I just played a tactical game and won comfortably. But I was under no illusions about just how unfit I really was. The British Open in April 1981 was my next major objective but, after talking with Cyril Carter, I decided to take up the offer of participating in *Superstars* and to use that multi-discipline event to improve my fitness.

By taking part in *Superstars*, I was following in the footsteps of Brian Jacks who had gained national recognition through his success in the series rather than through the medals he won on the judo mat. I recognised then and now that judo is a minority interest sport and with only six or so major competitions a year, cannot really sustain the interest of the Press and television. But I felt I was already fairly established in the minds of the sporting public, and that a successful appearance in *Superstars* would only enhance the public's awareness of judo and so I was determined to do well.

It all started easily enough: having been introduced to canoeing (Cyril Carter was at the time National Rowing Coach), I now came to grips with cycling, gym-tests, shooting, and basketball as well as specific track work for the 100 metres and steeplechase, and the obstacle course. As a 'skills' animal, I was in my element and as I mastered each discipline my hunger for training grew and grew and started to be reflected in my enthusiasm on the mat. The *Superstars* competition itself fell between the British Open Championships and the European Championships but Cyril and I had decided to train through the British Open when normally I would have 'peaked' and even to disregard the results of the European Championships (which turned out to be a wise move) and aim for the first real objective, the 1981 World Championships. Initially, the plan seemed to work well. My fitness improved and I won my heat of *Superstars* convincingly, winning six of the eight events outright. But then I suffered the second major injury of my judo career.

I had been feeling some pain in my left knee for quite some time but had put it down to the sort of twinges everyone experiences when they resume serious training after a lay-off. I suppose I was also reluctant to admit to any injury which would stop my build-up for the 1981 World Championships. The pain grew gradually worse until I was forced to seek medical advice. It was a problem with the cartilage in my knee; I knew it was, and the doctors confirmed it, yet I still postponed the initial appointments with the specialist in the hope that it might clear up. Eventually, I saw the specialist at Charing Cross Hospital and he convinced me that an operation was necessary to investigate the problem and possibly to remove the cartilage.

I must admit that my first reaction was fear and panic. Not only did I fear for my chances in 1981, but I was also scared stiff of the operation. Knee and back injuries are problems common to many top judo players and this is one of the main reasons why Cyril insisted that, wherever possible, I should avoid running on hard surfaces or hill running. Having noted the removal of all the cartilages in Brian Jacks' knees over the years and the sheer agony involved, I counted myself lucky never to have fallen foul of such an injury. However, one thing that a judo player can never avoid is the grinding pressure placed on the cartilage in his knees when twisting in and throwing an opponent, and the many years of competition had found the weakness in my knee.

I entered hospital full of trepidation, but the specialist assured me that he would employ the latest techniques, including an arthroscope which is a fibre optic tube through which he surveys the damage and a laser which can be used to destroy any irreparably damaged tissue. I awoke from the operation to find my knee swollen to the size of a football and to be told that part of the cartilage had been removed, leaving a small hole requiring only a couple of stitches. I would be out of hospital in two days, but the British Open was only five weeks' away.

I lay in my hospital bed and resolved that 1981 would still be my year and, more than that, I would still enter the British Open even if I had to throw everyone with my walking sticks. It was a crazy decision really but Cyril could see that I was determined and, two days after leaving hospital, he threaded me into a canoe and I started to work on my endurance and upper body strength. He programmed my training totally in a canoe and, believe me, it was really tough. It had to be as it was only seven days before the British Open that I was capable of stepping on to a judo mat. After miles and miles of canoeing at various levels of intensity and only three judo practices, I entered the British Open Championships.

I was only 60 per cent fit but I was hungry to get back on the mat. Another British competitor, Densign White, from Wolverhampton, was fighting in my weight category at the time and I knew that he would be the man I would have to beat; I also knew that he had been training extremely hard in order to defeat me at these Championships. We arrived at Crystal Palace about an hour before the start as usual and started suppling up before the first contest. I remember that I particularly enjoyed getting

Not all victories are as easy as this, but the Finnish policeman Seppo Myllyla wasn't going anywhere in the 1981 British Open Championships, though he gave me a tougher fight in the European Final in Paris in 1983

back into the familiar routine of competition preparation and I was so keyed up that I couldn't resist armlocking and strangling Cyril each time he attempted to stretch my legs!

All the contests up to the final that day went brilliantly well. I was back to my 1979 form and threw everyone for a full point. I knew that I would meet Densign in the final contest and that he was well schooled in all my major techniques and would be watching me closely throughout the day. With this in mind, I purposely avoided using ippon-seoi-nage with the intention of saving it up purely for Densign. The final didn't go as well as I had wished, for my ippon-seoi-nage scored a koka only, but I was satisfied that at least I had won the British Open Championships again – and against all odds.

Three weeks away were the European Championships in Hungary, and I was feeling confident despite the fact that Cyril and I had agreed to train through it with our sights firmly set on the World Championships. I won all my fights in Debrecen up to the semi-final quite comfortably and was convinced that I was on my way to another European title. Then there occurred a series of the unfairest decisions that I had ever suffered in the whole of my competitive career. The first happened when I was fighting Novotny of Czechoslovakia in the semi-final. I was a yuko up and had threatened on several occasions to armlock him on the ground when, immediately before an attack, he pushed me out of the contest area. The referee gave me the highest penalty possible without disqualifying me, a keikoku. As Novotny was an extremely defensive fighter and there were only seconds remaining, I stood little chance of throwing him for waza-ari or ippon and I had lost my opportunity to win the European title. I don't think I have ever been more cruelly cheated of victory. My spirits were low when I had to face Khabarelli of the Soviet Union for the bronze medal. I pulled myself together and was dominating him, with two kokas on the scoreboard and only a little contest time left, when exactly the same thing happened, and once again, I was given a keikoku penalty. I was completely devastated. This was the only major Championships in which I had failed to return with a medal. Even so, I learnt a valuable lesson and one that is vital to every judoka. If you play tactically close to the edge of the contest area, then you can easily get caught out by the rules. Such brinkmanship is a dangerous game to play and one which should be avoided if at all possible. Despite this apparent setback, I became even more determined that I would win the World Championships and returned for four months' solid training and preparation in London.

By that time another chapter in my life had already opened, one that was to result in more drama and more highs and lows than almost anything I

For a while, Sharron and I were the most photographed couple around

had ever known including those of international judo competition: my relationship with Sharron Davies. I had met Sharron at a Sportswriters' Dinner in London shortly after the Olympics, and after I had left Helen. It was, without question, one of those highly charged first meetings. Actually, it wasn't our first meeting because we had met briefly in the Olympic Village in Moscow but then we had both been consumed by a professional singleminded dedication to the work we had to do. In the relaxed atmosphere of a post-competition dinner in London, however, we were able to notice each other for the first time. We talked throughout that meal and we left together. If we had planned a secret affair, we couldn't have chosen a worse place to meet for everyone who was anyone in sports' journalism was there, and it didn't take long before the cameras started clicking and the gossip writers scribbling. For me, it was a totally different world.

Sharron has an extraordinarily strong personality for as well as being a talented sportswoman – she was one of Britain's finest swimmers of her day – she is energetic to the point of being tireless and extremely volatile. She was, and still is, zany, absolutely zany, and life with her was as unpredictable as it could ever possibly be. She loved the sparkle and the glamour of the public affair and I can only admit that at the beginning I enjoyed it too, for at last I was getting the public exposure which I felt my judo achievements had entitled me to, and which, I hoped, would result in the kind of public profile which would stand me commercially in good stead, at least when my competitive days were over. I had no idea how much of a double-edged business it would all prove to be, for at the time, the situation regarding trust funds and amateur status was not as clearly defined as it is now, and in the event I nearly got into serious difficulty from various appearances; and fairly quickly, I found the more callous newspaper interest intrusive in the extreme and the rudeness and insensitivity of so many reporters and photographers – 'Hi, Neil, hold on to Sharron and do your favourite kick' – irritating beyond belief. It was later to seriously affect our relationship but at first it was mildly amusing. But then everything seemed amusing in those early months.

Shortly after we met, I moved into the flat in Crystal Palace that Sharron shared with the gymnast Suzanne Dando and I learned to live in a state of constant unpredictability. The day after we met, we zoomed up to Leamington where she met my parents and life with Sharron was always like that – doing crazy things on the spur of the moment. One night, at 10.30, she decided that we had to set off for Ireland to buy a Great Dane – and we did exactly that, investing in a beautiful Dane called Benjamin who later, along with a boxer and a terrier, became quite a hallmark of the Sharron Davies/Neil Adams entourage as we toured the country making appearances, opening shops and fêtes and giving judo and swimming demonstrations.

For the first 18 months of our relationship, life was exciting, particularly as my judo was going well, but the seeds of our future problems lay in the very qualities that had first brought us together. First and foremost was the difficulty that I was still competing and therefore had to subject myself to the rigours of regular and singleminded practice, whereas she had retired. At the beginning, we used to go out running together because Sharron still wanted to keep fit; but when she was finally stripped of her amateur status – in a particularly shameful manner by the ASA, after she had attained the Commonwealth qualifying time with a fine swim – her interest in maintaining a high level of fitness understandably diminished. Her capriciousness was also difficult to live with because I think that at heart I need a steady home environment. I enjoy doing crazy things, but Sharron would drive me mad. I am soft-hearted really and will take a great deal but after a while pressure begins to build up and build up and then I will blow my top. It has happened only once on a judo mat in recent years, when I was practising up north somewhere, and another black belt began hacking at my feet. After a few kicks, I suggested that he should stop doing footsweeps until he learned how to do them properly but he continued in an unnecessarily unpleasant way until I completely lost my temper and had to be dragged off him. There are not many people who can drive me to the edge like that but Sharron managed it on a few occasions. I would never have hit her because I was frightened of losing control and she knew that really, and used to play on it. On one occasion I exploded, and threw a kettle through a window pane, on another, I put my fist through a wall, but that was part and parcel of life with Sharron. Looking back, I wonder if we were ever at ease with each other.

By the time I moved into the last phase of preparation for the World Championships, Sharron and I were living on our own in the flat in Crystal Palace as Suzanne Dando had moved out. It was partly, I think, because Sharron and I were so much a couple that life began to be a little uncomfortable for her and partly because she was going for the same work as Sharron. Our relationship was still at the relatively idyllic stage, my build-up was going fairly smoothly and I felt that with a reasonable draw, I could win the World's. A Briton had never been in the final of a World Championships before, so even that would be a first, though not good enough for me.

The World Championships took place during September in Maastricht which is a small, friendly town in Holland. My Japanese opponent from the USA Open, Jiro Kase, was there and I remember the look on his face when he found out I was fighting in the U78s. I found out later that the Japanese squad were discussing the prospects of either Katsuki (U71k) or Kase (U78k) meeting me at these Championships and that they were uncertain as to which category I would enter. Of course, when they found out, they all began to taunt Kase and I was confident, having already beaten him the previous year, that a good draw would see me through to the final which if I met Kase I would win. However, despite my confidence, I was still well aware of how lethal a Japanese player could be in a final of this standing and the World title at this weight had always been held by Japan. My draw was difficult but I think, of the two of us, Kase had a harder passage to battle. Still, I was happy and I couldn't wait to get started.

I was surprised to see that my first fight was against Davadaali of Mongolia who was the bronze medallist behind me in the U71k category at the Moscow Olympics. I knew he was an awkward and difficult player to fight and that he was also another of those dreaded extreme left-handers. When I got hold of him I was shocked by his sheer physical strength and I remember thinking how tough the competition was going to be. For the first couple of minutes, I was rattled and he, knowing my ability, fought off my attempts to get a grip on his right sleeve which made life even worse for me. Eventually I settled down, started to play my own brand of judo, and found that I was starting to pick holes in his defences. Suddenly I caught him with a well-timed kouchi-gari, which tumbled him over for a yuko score and I leapt on his back to follow it up with the juji-gatame roll. He really was extremely strong but I was surprised how easily his arm came out and he tapped his submission. A good start and a good man down – I felt optimistic.

My second contest was against Baptiste of Brazil which was probably the easiest of the competition. He too, was awkward, but no danger at all. Several times I nearly scored with the left seoi-nage and I couldn't help feeling that at any moment he was going to be thrown for a full point. My right uchi-mata brought a koka score and the kouchi-gari brought another. However, these were the only scores and the contest went to time but of course Baptiste was happy to have lasted the full course. The third fight was against Latrech of Algeria which proved to be a contest of brinkmanship, with each manoeuvring the other towards the edge of the contest area before beginning our techniques. I felt that it was only a matter of time before I would catch him and promptly scored a waza-ari with my ouchi-gari. After attempting an uchi-mata, I manoeuvered him to the edge of the area and suddenly, with a sweetly-timed osoto-gari, he was fiat on his back for a cracking ippon.

So to the semi-final, where I was to face a really difficult opponent in Kevin Docherty of Canada. But I had a distinct advantage in that my quarter-final fight with Latrech, which had lasted only two and a half minutes, was immediately followed by a real battle between Docherty and Barron (United States) which went the full distance. This meant that Docherty had only seven minutes' rest before meeting me on the mat. I was desperate to get on the mat as fast as possible as the less rest he had, the better for me.

Docherty is another extreme left-hander but I dominated his grips right from the beginning and threatened to unseat him with my initial seoi-nage and kouchi-gari attacks. Again, I felt it was just a matter of time and, two minutes into the contest, I devastated him with a kouchi-gari to score a waza-ari, and clawed after him to apply the juji-gatame roll. Unfortunately, he groped his way over the edge of the area and escaped the impending ippon. With one minute of the contest remaining, he started to make a last-ditch attempt but all I had to do was block him and I would be the first Englishman ever to reach the finals of the World Championships. The hooter sounded and that was it. I was in the final and I felt elated.

Tony Macconnell – a marvellous motivator and the best mat-side coach in Britain – encouraging me during my 1981 World Championship Final with team member Chris Bowles

On the other side of the draw, Kase had had a more difficult time facing Anatrovia (Soviet Union) and Petrov (Bulgaria) to reach the final. He only just made it, but would nevertheless be a typically awesome Japanese in the final of a World Championships. The British team manager at the time was none other than Brian Jacks and as I walked out for the final, he stopped me at the side of the mat and told me to forget everything, ignore everyone, and concentrate on this one fight. I could understand what he meant because there was a large British contingent in the stadium at Maastricht and it would have been easy to be distracted by yells of advice from the crowd. So I followed Jacks' advice. I was more confident as we bowed to one another than I can remember being for any major final I had been in up to that date and a different person from the one who had walked on to the mat of the Olympic final against Gamba. The instant I took hold of Kase, I knew I could win the match. In the opening seconds, I hit him with a near-perfect uchi-mata which would have sent anyone other than a Japanese crashing over for a full point win; his legs literally did a full split to get out of it but he was 'rattled' and it was a brilliant start.

I proceeded to open him up with seoi-nage before hitting him with tai-otoshi, which I had defeated him with in the USA Championships. He expected this attack, however, and virtually flung himself on top of me, so that we ended up with me on my back and him between my legs, in a perfect position for me to perform another variation of juji-gatame. He fell for it as planned and as the crowd were shouting 'Heave' I was pulling at his arm for all my worth. Unfortunately, I wasn't gripping his arm quite right but I strained as hard as I could in my attempt to apply bone-cracking pressure. In the end, the referee called 'matte' and stood us up again, with Kase rubbing his arm furiously. I had hurt him!

The crowd were going crazy as we battled for grips again and I launched into ippon-seoi-nage with all the speed I could muster. Kase went over, for what I thought was a score, and I pounced on his back for the juji-gatame roll. I first attacked one side and then switched to the opposite direction into the roll. We tumbled over and over three times and each time he slipped his head from under my leg. Eventually, he settled on to his back and, like all supple Japanese players, he attempted to bridge out of my grip. At this point, I remember concentrating on his arm and thinking, 'tighten your legs'. I gritted my teeth and fought to force his arm

In the first seconds of the 1981 World Championship Final against Jiro Kase only exceptional Japanese suppleness prevented an immediate victory for me – though ippon eventually came with my armlock

up towards his head just far enough to break his grip but not so far as to allow him to bridge out and escape.

We were on the floor for what seemed like an age but in reality it was only about 40 seconds; I was desperately trying to get his hand out and I remember seeing his fingers starting to pull and slide and I could see they were losing their grasp as you can tell when it's going to happen. I kept thinking 'You've done it, you B......, you've ...... done it! After his fingers had released, and I was trying to put the armlock on, I suddenly thought 'Oh God, he's not going to tap!' Then, when I saw his little hand come up and he tapped, I could have kissed him – but, of course, I didn't! At last I was Champion of the World; I raised my arms in triumph as the British contingent popped their champagne corks.

I lost control entirely and leapt around the mat like a demented baboon; when I got back to England, Cyril remarked that I was a World Champion who couldn't even clap his hands together for I kept missing every time. But it was fabulous, and I couldn't have cared less about anything at the time. After so many near misses, I was no longer a bridesmaid, I was number one! When I eventually got to the side of the mat, there were tears all round and I was sobbing uncontrollably. I didn't really know what to do. I just couldn't pull my tracksuit on fast enough to get to the rostrum, but because I was still sweating, I couldn't get it on which was irritating me, and everyone kept saying, 'Calm down, calm down!' Eventually, I managed to get ready and lined up for the medal ceremony and I remember thinking about the number of times I had already lined up in the queue. Of course, it was my turn to be second in the line, so that I would stand behind the number one spot; I couldn't help but assist Kase to his place in front of me, thinking 'Get in front of me, boy' and as we paraded for the medals I knew I'd done it then. By the time I'd stood on the rostrum and received my medal, the majority of British supporters in the crowd were already three-parts drunk. I remember that when they played the National Anthem, everybody was singing about six bars in front – it was fantastic, and all I could do was cry. Number One at last!

5

COPING WITH SUCCESS

My first act after winning the World Championships and enjoying the post-contest celebrations – and what celebrations they were! – was to make a serious error of judgement. At 23, I was still young and in certain ways impressionable, and not accustomed to the complex and untrustworthy world of commercial promotion. I knew the judo world intimately, the people involved, the sleights of hand that take place, the unspoken influences that persuade a referee to make this or that decision and all the tricks of the contest trade. I have always felt that it was a perfect microcosm of the outside world, but I hadn't quite understood the short- and long-term implications of being a 'sports personality' with all the agents, the well-meaning and less well-meaning hangers on, contracts, commitments and the thousand and one other details that accompany such a lifestyle. I thought I knew the rules but I found out the hard way that however skilled I was on a judo mat, or in *Superstars*, or even how I conducted myself at a shop opening or a judo demonstration, I was a complete novice when it came to choosing the people in whom I was to place my trust. In short, I made mistakes, signed papers I should never have signed and trusted people I should have viewed with caution. My involvement with the sports promoters had started before the 1981 World Championships, developed as Sharron and I became a 'media commodity' and culminated in something I have always regretted.

The morning after the final, I got into a car with Brian Jacks and Sharron – who had come to watch – and we drove straight back to London for a promotional event which was so unimportant that it is not even worth mentioning. It was something that neither Brian nor I should have even contemplated. Brian should never have left the team, which was still fighting as the U65k and U71k competitions were taking place the day after mine, and I should have spent the rest of the Championships encouraging my team-mates and generally enjoying the international atmosphere. Instead we made a rush for the Channel boat, and I missed the particular pleasure of post-World Championship success.

After the World Championships, I stopped training seriously for a couple of months though I did a little judo. It was the longest time I have ever had off and though I enjoyed it, I grew bored in the end and just wanted to get back to work. But it was very difficult to get back into training. I think that that was the only time that I became really big-headed and I had to severely take hold of myself. I had spent two months making the odd appearances and basically doing silly publicity stunts. Eventually, I gave myself the short-term goal of the Austrian Open which made me knuckle down to some training again. But like the USA Open the year before, I was nowhere near as fit as I should have been. I was treated differently at the Austrian Open because for the first time I was fighting as World Champion and I had become *the* target. Most of my opponents now didn't set out to beat me, but just to last full time with me which they felt was an achievement.

I won the Austrian Open but not particularly well. I beat Berthet of France in the final by holding him down but my arms were so tired they felt as if they were nearly dropping off. In the following months, I corrected my fitness problem, but the difficulties of sustaining the reputation of World Champion could not be dealt with simply in the weights room or by pounding the park paths. I had had years of preparation of living with pressure but what I was to encounter now was quite different. Being a National Champion, and even a European Champion, still leaves some room for manoeuvre and allowances are made for some margin of error. But as World Champion, a mantle of infallibility is placed on your shoulders, not just by others but even by yourself at times. It is a heavy mantle and it really cramps your style: particularly if you are trying to move with lightness, speed and imagination around a judo mat. I felt I couldn't possibly lose because I had a certain status to maintain. Every time I stepped on the mat, people in Britain would watch to see if I would be brought to my knees. Every time I went abroad with the British team, the Press and the judo world presumed that they had won at least one medal. Over the ensuing months and years, I became used to living with that pressure and to coping with it which is part of the responsibility of being a World Champion – but it didn't make it any nicer.

The closing months of 1981 and the start of 1982 did see changes in my lifestyle. For a start, Sharron and I moved into a new house in Addington, near Croydon. In theory, we were splitting the costs equally, but in reality Sharron was paying most of the bills simply because she began to make a lot of money, though that was further into 1982 and stretching into 1983. In contrast, I was still training and had very little income and that mainly from the Sports Aid Foundation. It wasn't easy for either of us, not because I am particularly conventional but because I want to pay my way, and Sharron understood to a certain extent. It was something that I couldn't help and we either had to live together and live like that for the time being or separate. It was as simple as that even though it was helped by the fact that she knew I was fairly generous with money, when I had it.

I also decided at this time that I would enter far fewer competitions. I had cut down already from the masses of domestic and continental competitions I used to enter, but I cut down further and, with Cyril, organised my training so that I would peak at prescribed times, just like boxers. In any case, 1982 was a relatively quiet time for me from a competition point of view. I won the British Open without too much difficulty and set my sights on the European Championships in Rostock, East Berlin.

Throughout my judo career, I had kept up-to-date not only with my opponents but also with the latest techniques. As I have already mentioned, judo has a huge number of different techniques and it has been said that even after 30 years of judo you can still go on a mat and see something completely new. That is not something that can be said about very many other sports. One of the new techniques which was becoming fashionable at the time was the yoko-tomoenage, the side stomach throw developed by the Japanese and which, incidentally, has been used with such skill by Kashiwazaki who taught at the Budokwai in 1983 for a year. I had found the throw technically interesting and, discovering that it fitted well into my pattern of movement, I had done some work on it. I used it throughout 1981 and regarded it as part of my repertoire of throws in 1982, though I hadn't really scored with it in international competition despite success with it at home.

The European Championships in Rostock went well until I met Shota Khabarelli, the Soviet Champion. His fighting style is completely opposed to mine as he favours an all-action grab, maul, push, pull, take-anything-you-can style which is something you just have to learn to contend with. I have never had any real difficulty with him (though one has to view all Soviet competitors with due respect) but he had beaten me previously when I received a penalty for stepping out of the area. This time, I was two kokas up when I tried the yoko-tomoenage, and was given a chui penalty (which overtook my score) for a negative dropping action. I went on to beat the Yugoslav Lescak for a bronze medal, for ippon with uchi-mata, but I was disappointed because again I felt I should have won the gold medal. There are quite a few European Championships which I considered I should have won, but I felt particularly strongly about that one; it was won by the Romanian Fratica whom I have almost always beaten with ippon.

Despite the slight European hiccup in championship success, I was beginning to benefit financially from the world title. I had been offered some small endorsements and a friend put forward the idea of making a judo video which would cover the 1981 British Open and World Championships. We called it simply *Ippon!* and though there were problems with it – the video quality was not very good and the commentary could have been improved though it wasn't too bad – I think it served a purpose. It was sold at far too high a price but it had some good quality shots from the final against Kase, especially the juji-gatame roll and my standing attacks, and I was glad to have a memento of those two events.

It was not until much later that I discovered I featured in another video prepared in 1982, which was the centenary year of the founding of judo by Kano. The Kodokan brought out a special video tape to mark the event, incorporating some rare historical material as well as shots of some of the leading Japanese judo figures in the twentieth century, including the 10th Dan, Mifune, Kano himself, Okano whom I particularly admired, Fuji, and the top fighters of the year, including Kashiwazaki and Yamashita.

Shozo Fuji of Japan, four times World Middleweight Champion, retired just as I entered the senior international scene; he is seen here at the 1975 World Championships in Vienna

Living judo history: Yasuhiro Yamashita, World and Olympic Champion, nine times winner of the All-Japan Championships, meets Anton Geesink, the huge Dutch World Champion who won the first Open Olympic title in 1964

Each one was chosen to demonstrate a particular aspect of judo but I was honoured to find that it was my juji-gatame which was chosen to demonstrate the application of kansetsu-waza. To give the Japanese credit, they showed in full the roll which put Kase on his back and the armlock which had meant the U78k title had been lost for the first time to a non-Japanese fighter. The Japanese can appear proud in many circumstances, but they do produce surprises like this.

I was also honoured in my own land in 1982 when I received the MBE for services to sport. It is a fairly standard government response to athletes who win world titles, but I was pleased nevertheless and, like most of my sporting colleagues who have been through the MBE ceremony at Buckingham Palace, I was impressed with the ease of manner and relaxed conversation of the Queen.

Increasingly in 1982, I found myself travelling around the country with Sharron as she supervised sponsored swims and made appearances of all kinds which I began to find more and more irksome. She was always recognised while I, who was still competing and had achieved just as much in my own field as she had in her's, was just the 'judo champion boyfriend'. Now when I look back, I can see things more clearly. She was a tall, blonde and good-looking girl and, of course, reporters and photographers preferred to ring her up and interview her rather than me; when we went out together, she was always recognised and people would come up and ask for her autograph and not for mine. Now I realise it is unimportant, but at the time it sickened my parents and really bothered me.

The year 1983 started well with one of my most enjoyable British Opens. I felt confident and relaxed and this was to mark all my competitions right through to the final of the World Championships in Moscow, but it manifested itself most clearly in the British Open. I did my normal range of tai-otoshis, juji-gatames and hold-downs and I think there was even a strangle as well but I was most pleased with my contests at the beginning and end of the day. On both occasions I fought a Mexican who was an absolute caricature of the egocentric Latin male. In the morning, he strutted around with his head in the air and was totally unprepared to be bounced up and spun round with an uchi-mata within seconds of the start. He landed heavily . . .

Somehow, it must have brought him down to earth mentally as well for he came second in the pool and we ended up meeting in the final, which was held on a mat streaked with afternoon sunshine. This time he came out more cautiously and tried to hold me off with strong arms. I did my standing armlock and it worked beautifully; he managed to jerk his arm free but spent the next five minutes writhing in agony while the rather helpless St John's Ambulance Brigade officers tried forlornly to do something about it. It was the Mexican's own fault for he should have tapped. When we restarted, he had changed his tactics and didn't try to keep me at arm's length any more which enabled me to step in with a real peach of an uchi-mata. We both took off, I turned him in mid-air, and he landed squarely on his back with a big exhalation of air. It was exhilarating.

As usual, I had a month before the Europeans, being held this time in Paris, but unlike most short pre-contest periods, it wasn't simply three weeks of training. For it was at this time that my club, the Budokwai, brought over Katsuhiko Kashiwazaki for a year's coaching. My admiration of the Japanese had never been unequivocal, though it is tempting because, after all, that is where judo originated, and I had never met Kashiwazaki. Of course, I knew him by reputation for he had won the U65k category in Maastricht the day after me and he had won the All-Japan Weight Category Championships five times which is no mean feat. Some people thought that I would feel slighted that another World Champion was coming to the club but nothing could have been further

Time fades the memory of many ippons, but not this one. Halfway through the final of the 1983 British Open Championships, I turned in on my Mexican opponent for a classic uchi-mata. He tried to stop it by clutching me around the waist, but I had already lifted him into the air with such spirit that both of us came off the ground to land with the Mexican squarely on his back

from the truth. I was looking forward to meeting him and I knew that anything I could learn from him would be to my advantage. The first time he came to the Budokwai, we met in the changing rooms, he nodded and we then shook hands. I think we were both a little apprehensive of the other.

Everyone grew to love Kashiwazaki in the end because he was just such a marvellous fellow. First of all, his judo was brilliant and especially his groundwork, for which he is renowned. It was a completely different style of judo from mine and I learnt a lot in those following months, particularly about the way in which he related his standing work to his groundwork. He was outstanding at turnovers and quite a few boys in the British team have now incorporated some of his moves into their repertoires. But it was not only his judo that made him so respected by everyone at the club but also his whole attitude because he wasn't typically Japanese. He was very warm and genuinely friendly. Of course, we practised with each other a few times and I loved it. I was a lot stronger than him because I was two weights up and he had retired from competition while I was approaching my peak, but he was still superb and very difficult to handle. I am sometimes very lazy because I am not often stretched in a club practice but Kashi, as we all called him, would goad me into action and make me work very hard. As I was still competing, I wasn't able to teach as much at the Budokwai as I would have liked, and Kashiwazaki revitalised the club while he was there. I saw him a lot during that time and found out many things about judo and Japan and judo personalities. I also discovered that he was much better at judo than at driving. He passed his test while he was in England but I don't know how!

One technique I learnt from Kashi and which I put into practice almost immediately was his kosoto-gari. I used to do something like it but his technique had one or two finer points which were worth incorporating into my own and I threw with it a couple of weeks later in the final of the European Championships, against Myllyla.

I love fighting in France because I know many French judo players and am familiar with the country, and also because their audiences are always so knowledgeable as well as large. Even so, I was gratified when I entered the Coubertin Stadium on 13 May – I am not superstitious in the least – and the packed French audience welcomed me with a standing ovation. I hadn't even done anything! But I enjoyed that event even though I felt I was just below par, having peaked a little earlier at the British Open. I easily beat a Belgian and a Norwegian and then I met an unknown West German, Frank Wienecke. He turned out to be an imposing six-footer, with all the arrogance and confidence of youth, and he wasn't bad either. I was never in any difficulty and I threw him for a small score but I was a little surprised when I rolled him twice into juji-gatame and was unable to straighten his arm. I noted how strong he was but didn't think much more about it. I was looking forward to meeting the Romanian, Mircea Fratica, who had won the European title the previous year and I went to town on him, armlocking him with, I confess, particular pleasure. Meanwhile, Seppo Myllyla, a courageous Finn, had despatched my great Russian rival, Khabarelli, and gave me quite a good run until he fell prey to Kashi's kosoto-gari and an ouchi-gari. It was my third Senior European title.

Despite Kashi's presence at the Budokwai, I was becoming slightly concerned that I wasn't obtaining the standard of practice I needed in England. We are a country that tends to produce outstanding individual judo players but we cannot boast depth and we just don't have as many players at grass-roots level as say in France or Japan. I discussed the situation with the new team manager, Colin McIver, who had taken over in 1982 and was to see us through the Los Angeles Olympics. He is very different from Starbrook, Macconnell or Jacks and is a tall and quiet Scot who had been the Scottish team manager and a friend of mine for many years. His approach was in stark contrast as he was very methodical in his preparation and did a lot of video research; he has proved popular with the boys even though he doesn't rely as much on personality as his predecessors. Eventually, we decided that in preparation for the World Championships in Moscow in September, I would spend a little time training in France and then a team of us would go to Japan at the beginning of 1984, in readiness for the Olympics.

And this was what happened. In between, however, I was persuaded to take part in the British Masters, the first competition of its kind to be held in the country, with invited teams from abroad. I still felt in good shape and after a testing fight against Brett Barron of the USA, which I won with a koka, when neither of us had really warmed up properly, I went through easily to the final to meet Andrzej Sadej of Poland. Sadej is a skilful and stylish player of no little ability – he had won a bronze medal in Maastricht – and we had an entertaining and open fight, until he tried a slow sacrifice throw which I simply side-stepped and then tied him up in kesa-gatame.

However, I hadn't really wanted to fight, because it meant an interruption to my carefully planned programme leading up to the World Championships in Moscow. There were also other complications. Relations with Sharron were coming to a head and for the first time in my career, I began to have time away from training for I can never train properly if I am feeling under pressure. I was distracted slightly by various possible commercial projects and the show-business side began to eat into my judo. Perhaps I subconsciously felt that because I had won my competitions so easily that year I could afford to coast a little. I had served my apprenticeship and all it needed was a couple of weeks to bring me up to peak, so even when I was training, I was just going through the motions. Even so, I felt confident when I arrived in Moscow because I thought I knew all the danger men who were likely to stand in my way of retaining the title, – all that is except one, Nobutoshi Hikage, the Japanese fighter. I knew he was good, that he had of course won the Japanese trials, and that he had come third in the All-Japan Championships – where there are no weight categories – behind Saito and Yamashita which is quite an achievement. I had also seen a couple of videos of him and I wasn't overly impressed. But until you take hold of someone on the contest mat, you have no idea what he is really like and, quite simply, I was in for a shock.

One of the problems was that I had come through my first four fights too easily but I could scarcely complain about the draw. I threw Luigi Nasti, a Neapolitan bank guard, with an ippon seoi-nage so hard that even I heard the thump echoing around the stadium. I then armlocked an Egyptian, Farid, and strangled my old Romanian rival, Fratica, with my favoured leg-strangle. My fourth fight lasted only 30 seconds because the Yugoslav Lescak kindly presented me with his back and I rolled and armlocked him with ease.

Hikage, on the other hand, had had a number of more difficult battles and therefore should have been tired when we met but he wasn't. I had no idea what he was going to be like. I had heard he was strong but I had no idea how strong and having watched his earlier fights, he didn't look terribly impressive. But as soon as I got hold of him I had a shock. I was expecting another Kase but it didn't happen. I realised I had a very different kettle of fish on my hands; he was just so much stronger. Still, I tried everything I could, but nothing seemed to penetrate his strength. Once I caught him on the ground and I heard Noboyuki Sato, the Japanese team coach, telling Hikage from the mat edge to stand up. Halfway through I was completely drained but thought I had done enough, and just had to play to get the decision, which I imagined I had done by the time the bell went. I couldn't believe it when one red flag went up for Hikage and one white flag for me. The referee hesitated for a fraction of a second and then gave the decision to Hikage. I was dumbfounded, and so was the crowd which booed and hissed at the decision as they clearly felt that lip-service was being paid to Japan.

However much I felt that I had lost to Gamba in the same stadium three years previously, I was convinced I had done enough this time. I can't remember Hikage making nearly as many big attacks as mine and even looking back at a replay on video I still feel the title should have been mine.

It made the following interviews with journalists difficult.

Gradually, as I gave the last interviews the stadium cleared of people and the cleaners moved in, which often gives the seriousness of championships a little worldly perspective for me, but I had to hang around to do a television interview which was to be screened on a sports programme the following day in Britain. Colin McIver, the team coach, had stayed with me throughout but we were looking forward to getting back to the privacy of our hotel. I gave the interview, and as I was speaking to camera, I caught sight of Kashi standing alone. Immediately I had finished and the camera crew had moved away, he came up to me and said in his simple English: 'Adam-san, I thought you won' and then just walked out. He had waited behind, missed all the coaches for the Japanese team, just to say that. That made him very special, but that was the kind of man he was.

At the time of the Moscow World Championships, I was 25 and with a number of major disappointments behind me, I had learned to cope with such incidents, but it was quite clear when I returned home that change was in order. Sharron and I had been spending most of the time at odds with each other, arguing and generally finding home life unpleasant. It was the year, 1983, when Sharron was finally stripped of her amateur status and that affected her badly but she had in any case been finding my continued involvement in top-level competition as galling as I had found her ability to attract attention. In truth, neither of us was made to sit patiently beside the other and sort out our problems. For our relationship to work, we both needed to have equal attention. The night I won my third Senior European title in Paris, I went back to the hotel to celebrate with some friends and members of the team and Sharron came with us. The talk was understandably all about judo and the fights of the day and Sharron felt rather left out, though in my own jubilation, I didn't notice it. Suddenly, I realised Sharron was no longer at the table. At first, we thought she had gone to the lavatory, but after half an hour, it was clear that she had disappeared in a huff, unable to take the neglect. I spent nearly an hour wandering around the streets near the hotel looking for her, until she eventually reappeared. It was typical of the kind of things that would happen though I could understand Sharron's point of view for it is not easy when you have competed at that level and suddenly it is gone – particularly when you stop competing as young as Sharron did. It was difficult for her to see somebody else on that special high when she knew that she would probably never experience it again. But, even so, that night in Paris should have been my moment and I wasn't allowed to enjoy it. Towards the end of 1983 we had begun to sleep in separate rooms.

6

LOS ANGELES

As November became Christmas and Christmas became the start of 1984, Olympic Year, the difficulties with Sharron and the loss of the world title, which still rankled, combined to chip away inexorably at my motivation to train well. It is not at all difficult for me to take it easily in England because unlike in Japan, there is no one really snapping at my heels, waiting for me to make the slightest slip to allow them to assume the top U78k spot. It is difficult to say without sounding immodest, but even at half speed, there is really no one to threaten me in Britain. Densign White, my 1981 British Open opponent, was the nearest I had had to a serious rival since Vass Morrison and by 1982, he was making the transition to U86k. By 1984 it was becoming clear that a young Scottish judo player, Martin McSorley, was showing real promise and each time I met him in competition, I found him a little more testing, but he still wasn't posing a real threat. And there was certainly no one who could push me to the limits in training. On paper, my plans to take me to Los Angeles looked as organised as always. I would fight four competitions that year only, the British Trials in January, the British Open in April, the Europeans in May and the Olympics in August, but I would 'peak' at the last two events only.

When I entered the Olympic trials at Crystal Palace, I was adrift psychologically. It felt like going to work – in the worst possible sense – and all I wanted to do was to get out of there as fast as I possibly could! Even when we were warming-up and suppling, I knew that it was going to be a bad day and this was confirmed in my first fight during which, despite scoring an ippon with sangaku-jime, I felt absolutely no desire to win at all. After that first fight, I knew I would have to summon all my concentration if I was to get through the day and from then on I decided not to chat with any of my friends and to focus, with Cyril, on each fight as it came. Despite the fact that I won every fight, except the final, with ippon, and despite all the congratulations and the obvious euphoria that herald Olympic year, we both knew that this had been the worst competition of my life. Normally, I use the trials as a warm-up even as part of my training and I go out to throw my opponents and try out new techniques and tactics. On that day, I couldn't have thrown my Granny! I won each of my contests on the ground, and in between, all I could say to Cyril was, 'I feel like I don't want to be here'. It felt really strange when people came up to us to offer their congratulations when we both felt that it was the blackest day ever. The final was a tense affair against young McSorley, who was Junior World Silver Medallist at the time, and I caught him only seconds before the bell with a sumi-gaeshi for which I was awarded yuko. There is no doubt in my mind that McSorley is one of the best British fighters I have encountered. He needs nurturing and he needs to come down to London and train as I did but his judo is good, particularly his standing work, though his groundwork is not bad either. But what's more, he has flair, is cocky, confident and has the will to win. He has that little bit extra and potentially is very good.

My fight with McSorley highlighted the fact that I just wasn't enjoying my judo in the least and if I was going to win anything at the Olympics, there had to be changes. These happened sooner than I anticipated. Sharron and I were continuing to argue and sleep in separate rooms but she came to watch me at the Trials. Towards the end of the day, she started to complain that I hadn't spent any time with her and I couldn't begin to explain that I had just had eleven fights and, though I had won them all, it was one of the most dismal days I had ever had so I just lost my temper and told her to go home. When I got back she was there with her father and I just sat down without saying much; her father and I got on pretty well. Then when he went something was said and I lost my temper again and that was the end really. We each went to our room and within a few days I left which was when the papers got hold of it.

I went to squad training the following Saturday and when I went back to our house in Croydon, the *News of the World*'s reporters were waiting there. I had gone to the house to pick up some things and as I ran up to the house, past the waiting newsmen, I said bluntly, 'Keep away from me'. It had been agreed with Sharron that there would only be the two of us, but when I got into the house, her father and some friends were there. So I just turned round and walked back out again. I went back at a different time to collect my belongings. An old judo friend of mine, Danny Daniels, rented out some student rooms and he said I could have a place for as long as I liked.

It was very hard at the beginning, going back again to a bed-sit after living in a very comfortable house but I was glad to get out and I needed to be on my own. At first, I thought I would just see whether I felt differently when things had calmed down, but after a week on my own, I knew I would never go back. My affair with Sharron was finished as far as I was concerned even though she didn't think I would stay away.

By this time, the papers were revelling in the situation and wouldn't stop pestering us. I said to Sharron, 'Just give them a story, give them what they want, just to get them off our backs.' I can't remember now which newspaper she eventually contacted, but it worked and for a while we had a little peace and quiet. And then I met Alison Walker, who was later to become my wife.

I knew Alison vaguely because she worked as a beautician in the Holmes Place Health Club near the Budokwai where I did much of my weights work and circuit training. One day, a few weeks after leaving Sharron, I was having a drink there after training with Stuart Williams, the U86k player who was a member of the British team that went to Moscow in 1983. We were at the bar when Alison came up to buy a drink for a friend and herself. They asked us to go and join them and we were just on a night out, so we went over and started to talk to them. Stuart was chatting up Alison and I was chatting up Alison's friend, but when we got up to go, I said, 'Right, Alison, I'll give you a lift home.' Stuart just looked at me and his chin nearly hit the floor. But I lived near Alison so it was quite sensible. I took her home, had a cup of coffee and then left. I said I would meet her the following evening, after training. Somehow, the word got through to the Press and though I didn't see them, the photographers must have been waiting outside the Budokwai, seen me leave and followed me to a local pub where I went to pick up Alison. When we came out, they started to take our photographs and, that night, rang up Sharron to get her reaction. Apparently they said, 'Did you know that Neil Adams has been seen with another girl leaving a pub?' She basically told them to get lost but then rang me to say that they had been pestering her. She was obviously very upset and kept on asking me to go back but I had to explain, as gently as I could, that it was finished. In fact, we are now good friends and I think we always will be.

Alison and I hit it off immediately. She was just my friend but I couldn't believe how well we got on. We had both recently finished relationships, which is one reason we may have got on well together, but though everyone warned us that it was just probably an affair on the rebound, we knew it wasn't. We started living together from the start really for either I was going to her place or she was coming to mine. Alison lived in Balham, so it wasn't too far away, and it was only a matter of time before we moved into a flat together.

If I look back on my personal life I can see that I haven't really been on my own, or at most, I have had a few months on my own. Perhaps it is partly because I like being looked after but I don't think that is the only reason. All three girls are marvellous people but my relationship with each was very different. My first was a kind of very young affair and Helen was a smashing person. Sharron was more of a raging romance type of thing. The Press built it up and it was a kind of sporty relationship but I still look at Sharron as a girl with a great talent who will always do brilliantly once she knows which direction she wants to head her life in. Alison I can't really explain. It is the end for me. As I said, she is a very close friend, and in fact, she is my best friend. I met her three weeks before I went to Japan for a month's training and during that time we wrote about 100 letters to each other. When I came back, we moved in together.

Colin McIver, the British team manager, regarded a month's training in Japan as a crucial part of the build-up to the Olympics. He felt it was important for the young boys in the team, such as Densign White and Kerrith Brown, who needed that kind of harsh experience if they were to realise their undoubted potential and get into medal positions in international competition and I suspect that in addition to feeling that it would sharpen me up, he thought it would be useful to get me away from the stresses of my private life. Of course, when the trip was organised, I was having difficulties but by the time the trip was imminent, my life had been sorted out and in some ways Japan was the last place I wanted to be. But I did recognise that hard training and high-quality practice was what I needed, and so I went with the team.

This time we stayed in a comfortable first-class hotel and it was cherry blossom time which also helped as it was just becoming warmer. And we needed every bit of help because most of the time we were absolutely exhausted by the training. We would get up in the morning and go for a run, but not too far, just three or three and a half miles, and then we could do what we wanted until the afternoon. At first, we used that time to do weights but later on we found the afternoon practices so tiring that we just rested. This was because the afternoon practices lasted for three hours or more, and if you weren't rested by the time the afternoon judo started, you would be thrashed on the mat. You just can't defend yourself when you get tired. The pattern was more or less the same in most of the dojos that we visited: we would warm up, then do uchi-komi and then we would practise for two hours non-stop. In the Kokushikan they alternated the newaza and tachiwaza practices and they just kept firing new opponents at you all the time. Once we were out for about 20 minutes, with the Japanese hurling fresh competitors at us the whole time, and though we were giving them some stick, we were receiving it too. Some of their top students there are pretty damn strong and they tried to set me up quite a few times but I watched carefully and would accept certain practices only, taking the hard ones now and again. If I didn't do that, I would have been on the floor, because we are just not used to such long practice sessions, and to be honest, I can't see the point in them. Inevitably, it sometimes did get out of hand, they would try to throw you against the wall and things like that, and you had to retaliate. That's just human nature.

I didn't think it was the best kind of training for me. I can do my strength and cardio-vascular work in the morning and then my hour and half of judo in the afternoon or evening which is enough for me. Maybe a couple

Colin McIver, 6th Dan and British team manager from 1982-85, has remained an active judo player himself as was seen when he accompanied the British team to Hungary in 1981

of hours but no more. Sometimes, I was bored on the mat because I had done it all before when I was 16 and the one thing that I didn't want was to be bored because I was having enough trouble motivating myself as it was. On the other hand, I was thrown out there in a way that I am rarely thrown in England. It is different, too, because nobody looks and gawps. The high technical standard of the Japanese means that if you are not sharp, you will be immediately thrown. I had a marvellous practice with a boy from Tokyo University. I would have beaten him in a contest any time, but because we were both loose and opening up, we threw each other. I may have thrown him more than he threw me but he caught me with a left uchi-mata which was a cracker.

Paradoxically, it is often the case that you need time to adjust from the hard but more classical Japanese style of judo to the more angular, opportunist European style and when I came back to England, just before the British Open, I didn't have that time to adjust. From the point of view of motivation, I felt better than at the Trials but perhaps I was a little over-confident too. I struggled against the Dutchman Henneweld and was caught for the first knock-down in competition in four years by an unknown Dutchman, Johann van Heeft, though I went on to beat him convincingly. In the final, I found it difficult to penetrate the defence of the West German Christian Siebald, whom I had thrown for ippon on our previous meeting, and had to rely on decision to win. Clearly, something had to be done to prepare myself for the European Championships in Liege, Belgium, and that meant not returning with the rest of the British team to Japan for a further month. I felt I could do better on my own in Europe which is what I did.

I 'peaked' for the Europeans as planned and certainly felt more confident and in control. The fluency and timing of my throws and groundwork was coming back slowly but surely and I had all kinds of judo styles thrown at me in Liege, in May. I threw and armlocked Finland's Jukka Metsola in 33 seconds and literally swept aside the bruising challenge of France's Michel Nowak with an opportunist footsweep. I had a tough semi-final exchange with the East German, Ramon Pink, who knocked me down with a counter for a koka; I then stepped up a gear, levelled the score with a footsweep and was unanimously awarded the decision. The final was the famous boxing match with the Hungarian Fogarasi just trying to slap me around while taking grips and eventually running up the penalties while I just kept cool. It was not an ideal performance in Olympic year, but an adequate one. At last I was starting to get some 'fight' back into me but I felt that I was a long way off the form I would need to show later in the year. After winning the European

Championships for the fourth time, I felt a psychological boost and decided that I would now enter a phase of 'power' training in order to build up the strength I would need to tackle the likes of Hikage. Over the past two years, I had shied away from using heavy weights purely because I hated the physical pain involved in such training and the subsequent initial loss of speed and control on the mat. I was very nervous about letting Cyril test me because I knew that I wouldn't show up very well. But after five weeks of sheer agony, I felt enormously strong and couldn't wait to get to the States. My confidence was high, my judo good and I was certain that with a good draw the gold medal, the pinnacle of my ambition, would be mine. I hoped that the poor beginning to the year was just a case of 'poor dress rehearsals mean a good first night'.

Just before I left, rumours started to circulate concerning who was going to be in my weight category at the Olympics. Hikage was out, as he had been beaten in the Japanese Olympic Trials, and a boy called Takano replaced him. I didn't know much about this Japanese but I wasn't at all worried about fighting him. A rumour had also reached us that Gamba had moved up into my weight category which I thought sounded absurd and which subsequently turned out to be false. The peculiar thing about an Olympic Games is that whereas in any other championships you can predict the top six competitors, even though the order of merit might change, in the Olympics you can only say that out of those six competitors, two are going to be in the top four and you can guarantee that one or two are going to be thrown up from nowhere. That's what the Olympic Games does; it creates special or 'freak' performances and it was really strange, in the light of what happened, that Cyril and I had discussed this very issue immediately before my departure for the States. We also talked about the players whom I would be fighting in Los Angeles. Of course there were the obvious contenders such as: Nowak (France); Takano (Japan); Fratica (Romania); Docherty (Canada); Barron (USA); and Henneweld (Holland); and we chatted at some length about their relative strengths and weaknesses. I also discussed Wienecke (West Germany) and I remember saying 'He's fast and he's strong but he tends to lose to people he shouldn't really lose to. I am not really worried about him. I was all over him the last time we fought.' I just didn't take pure chance into account.

When we arrived in Los Angeles, the temperature was 90 degrees Fahrenheit in the shade and it was obvious that the heat was going to be a real problem and something we would have to get used to. The first thing I noticed was the massive security which constantly surrounded us and was far more obvious than it had been in Moscow. But the atmosphere was extremely pleasant and everyone was friendly and polite. We were staying at the campus of the University of California in Los Angeles which was on the outskirts of the city and set in a beautiful part of the countryside. The only problem with staying at the university was that there was no indoor judo hall available; the nearest one was at least 90 minutes away which meant it would be a full day's work just to get an hour's practice.

So instead, we decided to train on some wrestling mats which had been placed inside some massive tents erected in the UCLA grounds. The tents weren't air conditioned and, with the temperatures soaring into the 90s, we struggled to maintain good quality practice. Nevertheless, I was generally pleased with the way my final preparation was going, though at one stage, we were doing a lot of shuttle running and my legs felt dead . . . so much so that I stopped running entirely in order to give them time to recover. Compared to the Moscow Olympics, the training and venue were much better and I was looking forward to fighting.

And so were the others. With Steve Gawthorpe (U65k) having won a bronze in the European Championships (when the Romanian Ilie Serban was strangled unconscious), and Neil Eckersley (U60k) and Nicholas Kokotaylo (U95k) having fought for bronzes in Liege, there was a real possibility that this team could bring back more judo medals than the silver and two bronzes obtained in 1972, particularly as any one of the rest – Densign White (U86k), Kerrith Brown (U71k), Elvis Gordon (O95k) and Paul Radburn (Open) – could produce the goods which is exactly what happened. By the time I went to fight, we already had two bronzes, one from Neil Eckersley and one from Kerrith Brown.

I couldn't wait to see the draw for my weight category in order to see who I was going to meet. I received this a week before I was due to fight, which gave me plenty of time to think about it and, possibly, too much. I was disappointed to see that I would be facing four of the top people in my weight category and that I was easily in the hardest corner of the draw. My opponents were likely to be Henneweld, Barron, Nowak and Lescak. Lescak was the least of my worries but I knew that I would probably have to face him in order to get through to the final. I had hoped for at least a couple of relatively easy initial fights before meeting tough opponents but it certainly wasn't going to work out that way. The opposite half of the draw looked much easier with Takano, Fratica, Docherty and, of course, the much-less fancied Wienecke. If all went according to form, I felt that I would face either Takano or Fratica in the final.

As the contest day approached, I grew more and more nervous though I was delighted that Eckersley and Brown had achieved bronze medals. I felt that the pressure on me to win the gold medal was enormous. Still, I had been in this situation before, so I wasn't really concerned by the all too familiar '747' in the stomach and I had already learned that adrenalin was coloured brown. I had my job to do and I was confident that I would do it.

My first fight of the day was against the winner of a contest between Henneweld and a player from the Dominican Republic, so we knew that it would be Henneweld. I had fought the Dutchman three times before, once scoring ippon from uchi-mata, second scoring ippon from an armlock, but on our third meeting I had scored two kokas only. I was always confident of beating him but I was concerned whether this contest and the next one to follow would last the full five minutes because I suspected that my hardest contest would come in the third round against Nowak. I wanted to be as fresh as possible before facing him.

I started off the contest with Henneweld by opening him up with several minor techniques which threatened to score. Then, having gained my favourite grip, I attacked him with right tai-otoshi which he attempted to escape by stepping over my extended right leg. I had collapsed on my right knee and, just as he was stepping over, I stood up swiftly and turned the movement into a seoi-otoshi which promptly spun him over for ippon. I was really pleased with such a fast and convincing win and my confidence received the boost it needed.

After a long wait, I found that my next fight was going to be against the winner of a contest between Brett Barron (USA) and a fighter from Kuwait. Once again, it was reasonably certain who the winner of that

---

Britain's three judo medallists from Los Angeles: Kerrith Brown, me and Neil Eckersley

match would be. I was possibly more nervous about the impending fight with Barron than with any other competitor at the Games, because I knew just how strong and difficult he could be; he always plays a tactical match using the edge of the area and, of course, he was fighting in front of his home crowd. There were about 5000 spectators for this fight, 4996 were supporting Barron and 4 (my mother and father, my brother Chris and Alison had come to watch me) were supporting me. I was also worried about the standard of judging and refereeing at these Olympics, knowing how close the result of this particular contest could be for it was obvious from some of the decisions made in other sports, such as boxing and gymnastics, that there would be an extremely heavy bias towards a competitor from the host nation. When we walked out into the contest area, the whole crowd seemed to be chanting for Barron and there appeared to be over 50 of his immediate family present at the side of the mat.

I had fought Barron on two other occasions and each time it had been a tough contest decided by a koka only. I suppose the chanting and general support for Barron turned my nerves into aggressive energy because when I got hold of him, I was determined that I would not allow him to play his 'spoiling' game and set my sights firmly on his left arm. He started off the contest quite predictably, by playing the edge, coming in for his left uchi-mata and falling on his face in order to avoid a counter. In that position, it was almost impossible to get him into groundwork, because he could easily manoeuvre us out of the area. I knew that if I could make him do the same attack inside the area, then I would be on his back like a leech for the juji-gatame roll. In fact, it was he who miscalculated an uchi-mata attack on the edge of the area and left me just enough room to pursue him on to the ground. I jumped on his back and immediately he desperately tried to roll outside the area. I managed to turn his head to a position where his attempt at rolling was bringing him back inside the area and, once I had rolled him onto his back into juji-gatame, I found that his arm straightened out fairly easily. I snapped on the armlock as vigorously as I could and he submitted immediately. Of course, my four supporters went berserk while the American crowd were shocked into silence but as I left the mat area, the crowd were more than generous in their applause. I met Barron in the village the next day, and discovered that my juji-gatame had been so vigorous that I had dislocated and fractured his elbow. I was upset by the idea that I had injured a worthy opponent and offered to be the first to sign his plaster!

I was pleased that I had finished these first contests in such a short time because I knew that my next contest, against Nowak, would be an extremely tough one. Nowak has the strongest pair of arms I have ever come across and I knew that in the first two minutes of this contest, I would have to weather a whirlwind of attacks and counter-attacks but I was confident that after two minutes, his endurance would run out and I would be able to start to pick him off.

As predicted, the Frenchman came at me like a bat out of hell. His right arm gripped me like a vice and he kept attacking me with a pick-up technique which generally resulted in him clouting me round the ear. Despite the viciousness of his attacks, I felt in absolutely no danger of being thrown by him. I gripped him right-handed as if I was going to throw him with tai-otoshi and as he stood upright next to the edge of the area I attacked him with tomoe-nage and scored a koka. Shortly afterwards, I attacked with kouchi-gari to go two kokas up. The contest went to time, and towards the end I felt my forearms seize up and my legs turn to jelly, but I was through to the semi-final.

Not even the bruising strength and hasty handstand of Frenchman Michel Nowak can stop himself falling for a yoko-tomoe-nage in Los Angeles. Notice my controlling right foot

As predicted, I had to face Lescak, whom I had fought twice before and had beaten easily with two ippons, one from an uchi-mata and one from an armlock. Unfortunately, this contest went to time purely because I didn't have enough energy left in my legs to attack properly, though throughout the contest I felt that I could throw him at will. Having caught him with both tai-otoshi and tomoe-nage to go two kokas ahead, and having almost taken his arm twice with juji-gatame, I was so tired that I was merely content to 'coast' through the rest of the contest. So there I was, through to my second successive Olympic final.

It was really strange that during the hour's wait for the final against Wienecke, I felt really depressed and somewhat more tired than I had ever felt before. All I could think was that I wanted to get these Olympic Games out of the way and I couldn't seem to pick myself up psychologically. What I should have felt at that time, I realise now, is that I wanted nothing more on earth than to be Olympic Champion, but I didn't feel motivated at all by this prospect. I suppose the pressure and nerves had taken their toll and I hit a tremendous low. Despite these feelings, I still felt confident that I would beat Wienecke quite convincingly.

Despite beating Takano, Wienecke was lucky to have even reached the finals, having got there by virtue of a split decision against Fratica. He had never even been placed in a top international competition before and I never regarded him for one moment as a threat. I knew that his techniques were right uchi-mata and left ippon-seoi-nage but I had fought him before and beaten him easily. As we stepped out onto the mat area, I felt extremely nervous as usual and my legs were like jelly. But I knew that Wienecke would be feeling exactly the same.

I started the contest by dominating his grips and achieving my own favourite sleeve grip and I felt in no danger whatsoever: in fact, he wasn't even attacking me during those first two minutes. I attacked him with tai-otoshi which was initially awarded a koka but then removed from the board and swiftly followed up with a kouchi-gari which again I felt should have scored a koka. But I had been counting as we were fighting and I knew I was seven attacks ahead of him and was winning easily. I thought it was only a matter of minutes before I would either throw him or go to the ground to win the contest. I remember looking at the clock and seeing 3 minutes 50 seconds had elapsed and thinking, 'Three minutes to go and you're Olympic Champion'; but it didn't quite work out that way. I had manoeuvred to a position where Wienecke was standing with his back to the edge of the contest area and he attacked with a very feeble, one-handed right uchi-mata which I squashed easily. I didn't even think that he was going to attack again as we were so close to the edge of the contest area but then he made a one in a million attack with left ippon-seoi-nage and, because of my stance in defending against uchi-mata, I felt myself being thrown over my fully extended and braced left leg. There was absolutely nothing I could do. I had miscalculated and had mentally shut off and was caught by what could be termed a 'sucker punch' only. I remember hitting the mat and thinking, 'Damn! he's got a waza-ari' but I looked around to see the referee standing with his arm raised firmly aloft for the full ippon.

Once again, I was left sitting completely stunned in an Olympic final while my opponent and his supporters went crazy. No one, least of all Wienecke, had expected this result and I just couldn't believe that it had happened to me again. I bowed and stepped off the mat in a daze and went to a small room downstairs to prepare for the medal ceremony. There was just Colin McIver and me and I fell on my knees and said, 'I just made a mistake, I can't believe what I have just done. I was winning so easily.' There was nothing more I could say. However, I was four years older than I had been in the Moscow Olympic final, and I had suffered other major

Two minutes into the Olympics final against Wienecke and I was confidently searching for groundwork openings with no idea of the defeat that was just around the corner

disappointments in between, so I was more able to accept defeat. I was still smarting from the pain of it, however, when I had to face the inevitable television cameras and was questioned about the validity of the ippon decision. But within a couple of days, I had realised that it was just one of those unpredictable occurrences and it was just unfortunate, not to say ironic, that after nearly 20 years of judo and having never been thrown for ippon in a contest, any contest, it happened in the final of the Olympic Games. I think Wienecke is going to have difficulty in sustaining that success because though I think he is good, very good, I am still convinced it was a chance event that could not be repeated in a thousand meetings between us. But he deserves the credit of being Olympic Champion, while my dream still has to be realised.

7

FIGHTING BACK

In the four years following the Moscow Olympics, I had had more than my share of triumphs and defeats so I was much more capable of dealing with the disaster of the Los Angeles final, and to put it into some kind of perspective. After all, I had done well in all my early fights, my conditioning and preparation work was paying off, and I even did quite well in the first couple of minutes of the final: for the rest, well, as the Japanese saying goes, 'even monkeys fall off trees'. So this time I was over the worst of the shock within a couple of days, not least because I had my family with me, and Alison.

Of course, everyone was wondering what I was going to do, whether I was going to call it a day and retire or go on fighting. The speculation in the Press and among the judo fraternity both in Los Angeles and back home covered just about every conceivable possibility. Would I retire or would I stay on for another World Championships? Would I go on until the next Olympics, perhaps even going up another weight category to U86k? Was I going to be like a punch-drunk boxer, hanging on for a slice of glory when way past his best or did I still have the ability to contest for the top medals? All these possibilities went through my mind too, but in the end the answer was very simple. I was 26 and probably only just reaching my peak. There was no reason why I should not continue, though for how long I don't know even now. By the time I came home, there was no doubt in my mind that my sights were set firmly on the World Championships in Seoul but first, there was another major event to prepare for and enjoy, my marriage to Alison.

Despite the clear decision on my judo future, it was probably fortunate that I had no time to sit and brood in the vacuum of the post-competition period for, when I arrived back in England, there were just two weeks before the wedding and much to be done. Throughout the traumatic last days in Los Angeles, Alison and I had become even closer and I have never got on with anyone as well as I have with her. In a way, we are both pretty easy going and like to live life without troubles or upheavals. That was very apparent in the time we spent together before the Olympics and it was one reason why I proposed within a month of meeting her. I learned to

TOP LEFT *It is not a strangle I would submit to on the judo mat but life is played by different rules. Alison and I celebrate after our wedding at St Nicolas Church, Asthall in Oxfordshire*

TOP RIGHT *Cyril Carter, my personal coach for many years, at my wedding*

love and admire her for many reasons, including her innate courage: in summer 1984, she had done a parachute jump and an awkward fall had resulted in crushed vertebrae which gave her a lot of pain and raised serious doubts about her future health. I am glad to say that now, with a lot of determination, she is regaining her fitness, and comes running with me as well as going to tap dancing classes. We had originally planned to get married before the Games, but in the end, with the wedding to be organised and my training to consider, we decided to leave it until afterwards.

Alison's father, Alan Walker, owns a large farm near Oxford and we were married in the Walkers' local village church of Asthall. It was a beautiful day, and the whole village, it seemed, came to the wedding. The reception was held in a restaurant Alan owns which is at the top end of the farm, in a converted barn, and we were driven there from the church in a vintage car. Our families wanted us to leave the reception in a way we would never forget, and though I didn't know it at the time, a complete catalogue of crazy ideas had been considered. At one stage we were going to be driven away in a Sherman tank until the one available developed some engine trouble. The next idea was a hot air balloon, but we were too near an RAF base, and hot air balloons need almost perfect conditions, so it was thought too risky. In the end, we came out of the reception to find, awaiting us in the drive, a Model T Ford motor lorry with a big brass double bed in the back. We climbed on the bed to the accompanying music of a jazz band and left in style, en route for Israel.

The two weeks we spent touring the country, where, of course, I had won my first international title and where I had been on a number of occasions since, was one of the most relaxed and enjoyable I can remember. Only occasionally did thoughts of yet another 12 months' hard build-up towards a major competition interfere with what was essentially a very happy time. One of the enduring difficulties of a competitive life is that you can never wholly relax, because part of your mind is always set on the next big event. This constant mental pressure is as wearing as the constant physical demands made on you and it is something you never quite totally come to terms with unless you are extremely easy going. I recently went out for a drink with my father and he asked me how long I was going to continue competing, and I had to reply that I honestly didn't know. He pointed out that I hadn't really led a normal life; I had never known a time when I didn't have to do something, to go out running, or to get to judo to train, or to watch what I was eating or drinking because I had a competition in a week's time where I would have to walk out in front of a crowd of 15,000 and fight someone of world-class standard. Even now, I find that to do that and still look calm takes all the courage I have. And I never know, until I step onto that mat, whether I am going to feel sharp and alert or, for some unaccountable reason, as weak as a kitten with legs like jelly.

Perhaps, I have never been totally relaxed in my whole life, though I am not complaining and it is better than working under a car with oil dripping on your head. But there is no doubt that sport is cruel. Judo is one of the world's great levellers and there have been times when I have paid for being too cocky, but the lessons I learned from the two Olympic finals I have fought in have been hard ones. They were my two major lessons or, if you include the 1983 World Championships, perhaps three. But you have to keep on bouncing back and perhaps I learnt more from losing than I would have by winning them. I shudder to think what I would have been like had I won all my big fights which I know I had the technical capacity to do: I don't like what I see in one or two other British World Champion sportsmen I have known whose constant success has made them arrogant and rude in a way which may be understandable in a young man but is unacceptable in someone of more mature age.

By the end of our honeymoon, my mind was beginning to stray to training schedules and judo and I was looking forward to getting back on the mat. My first objective was the Trials at Crystal Palace in December and just how unpredictable sport and judo is can be seen by comparing my performance in December 1984 with the first competition of the same year in January, the Olympic Trials. For the January competition, I was sluggish, bored, and capable of going through the motions only, allowing my experience to win everything on the ground. How different, then, were the December Trials! I was bubbling over with enthusiasm, really enjoying it and experimenting, as I normally do at the Trials, with new techniques. I had eleven contests that day and won all with ippon, accumulating four throws, four armlocks, two hold-downs and one strangle, which is not a bad spread of techniques. In my last fight I met Richard Armstrong whom I had fought on many previous occasions. Our last meeting had been in the Olympic Trials and I had had a hard time against him, only catching him with an armlock in the last 30 seconds. This time, despite having had ten fights beforehand, I took hold and threw him for ippon with uchi-mata in eight seconds. I don't remember anything about that uchi-mata – I couldn't tell you whether it was a spinning entry or a catch-up – because it just happened. The best judo is usually when there is nothing pre-meditated about it and instinct is allowed to take over and produce something outstanding. Most of the time, you do draw opponents into traps, but the best victories are when you are looking down at someone who is lying on their back and in a way you have no idea how they got there.

That is why you have to develop a certain philosophical attitude towards judo and sport and life. I could not begin to explain why I was on such good form at those Trials, or at Maastricht in 1981, and why the events in Moscow and Los Angeles happened. That is one of the great mysteries of life for me. Even if you fed all the data into a computer, you still wouldn't come out with an answer – the computer would probably blow up. Not even a computer can describe the infinite permutations that go to make up one human being's performance on one day. All you can plan for is that, by diligent training, you can raise your minimum standards.

The Trials did make one thing conclusively clear to me. At 26, I was certainly not physically past it. Unevenness in my performances at championships could partly be put down to my training and whether it has gone smoothly or not but my mental attitude at this stage in my career was the most important part of all. From now on, taking technical preparation and physical fitness as a constant factor, my success, I was convinced, would be a direct reflection of my mental state. That is why in January 1985, it was imperative that my first task was to walk into the lion's den of the West German Open and face Wienecke on his home ground. Most of the emotional shock of the disastrous Olympic final had passed and yet Wienecke as a fighter still hung over me. Although this was less important to me now, I had to prove to myself and perhaps to the world that the ippon-seoi-nage had been a fluke; and that Wienecke, as a strong but not outstanding opponent, had to be put into perspective in the international arena.

Having decided that I was going to the West German Open, which was at the end of March, my mind suddenly cleared. I discovered I was eager to train and eager to practise; I was looking at my judo afresh, working on yet more groundwork moves and sharpening up my standing work. I sped through the early rounds of the West German Open and then faced a little-known Pole, Waldemar Legien. I took hold of him, threw him in 15 seconds for ippon with tai-otoshi and dismissed him from my mind, little thinking that we would meet two months later in the final of the European Championships.

But then my mind was really concerned with the final against Wienecke. This is what I had come to Germany to do and, though confident, I was also more nervous than I should have been. Perhaps that was why I didn't fight particularly well and why it was eventually settled by a decision. There was no question about which way it would go for Wienecke had hardly made any attacks and he was obviously pleased that he had lasted the full time. But I was annoyed because I didn't beat him by a full point which I knew I could do. Of course, it wasn't easy for him. He had had a difficult few months, trying to live up to the reputation of being the only man ever to have put me on my back and, frankly, it was something he could never really live up to because he cannot be ranked higher than fourth in the world, behind whoever the Japanese and the Russians put up, Nowak and me. This showed at the next event, the European Championships in Hamar, Norway, where he lost in the first round to the East German Torsten Oehmigen.

When I returned from the West German Open, I went to see my father whom I hadn't seen for a while and it was he who suggested that I slightly change my training routine for the Europeans. He is the one person I have listened to throughout my career and on this occasion I took his advice to heart. In the weeks before the competition I drastically reduced my conditioning training and instead worked for hours in the Budokwai's dojo with Ray Stevens, on sharpening my entry into throws and ground-work moves. It was gratifying to see that Ray's judo had developed enormously through the work we did with each other. He had won a bronze medal at the Multi-Nations in Paris (and that is a bronze medal worth having because it is one of the hardest of European competitions), had continued to show extremely good form, culminating in a silver medal in the British Open, thus earning himself a place in the British Team for the European Championships. For me, it was a perfect example of Kano's dictum that judo should be of mutual benefit – to yourself and others.

So Ray and I both worked intently and uninterruptedly for Hamar, and though it proved an unsuccessful event for Ray, it showed that my mental and physical preparation was spot on. Hamar is a small town in the centre of Norway, situated beside the large lake of Mjosa, and though it was May, there was still snow in the pine forests and the lake was frozen. The competition took place in a sports hall which was more like a converted aircraft hangar and the atmosphere seemed more domestic than international yet it was altogether a friendly occasion – and an extremely satisfying one for me. I threw and armlocked the Swiss Olivier Schaffter and then strangled the Yugoslavian Lescak, which put me into the semi-final against the new Russian, Vladimir Chestakov. This 24-year-old, who had supplanted my old rival Khabarelli, had won the Tiblisi tournament with ease so he was not to be taken lightly – especially since he had armlocked Michel Nowak which I have never done! But I felt quietly confident, and after about two minutes, threw him with tai-otoshi for waza-ari, faked an armlock attempt and caught him with a variation of sankaku-gatame that I had been working on.

The final was almost a replay of the 1984 European Final, when the Hungarian Fogarosi had spent the whole contest breaking grips. This time it was Legien who decided to try the same tactics, just to last to the end of the contest, rather than to throw me. I only once got both hands on him in the grip that I needed and I immediately threw him with tai-otoshi for yuko. It was so fast that he actually over-spun, otherwise it could easily have been ippon, but I couldn't risk a more considered attack with his grip-breaking tactics. I said after the competition that it was the first occasion that I felt I had given a world-class performance for some time. It was partly due to a change in those last two weeks of training but mainly because I felt a lot better in myself: I wasn't under a lot of public pressure and there were certainly no pressures at home. So mentally, I was on top form; for me, judo is a mental battle. If I could get my mind right, I would be ready for the World Championships in Seoul.

Autumn 1984 opened a new chapter in my judo life. Up to the arrival of Kashiwazaki at the Budokwai in May 1983, the two senior instructors who had taught regularly at the club were Syd Hoare and Tony Sweeney, both of whom had been prominent figures there from the time I first arrived. The purpose of inviting Kashiwazaki was to inject a breath of fresh air into

Even in a punch up – which the final of the 1984 European Championships indisputably was – you can still work technically. Here, only a fraction of control was missing for a good kouchi-gari on Waldemar Legien

the Budokwai and it certainly succeeded. However, his departure in April 1984 to teach at the new International Budo University in Chiba left a gap at the Budokwai. I was formally asked to become chief instructor, which I was glad to accept, but it was clear that I wouldn't be able to give the job its necessary commitment until after the Olympics. So, initially, I relied heavily on other instructors at the Budokwai – particularly Peter Blewett and Kevin Crickmar whom I had known for many years – to take some of the load and prepare the way for what was really a new phase in the club's history.

Judo clubs inevitably go through good and bad times: when I arrived in London, the Budokwai was with the Renshuden pre-eminent among London's judo clubs but by the beginning of the 1980s, while its randori nights were popular, it had lost a strong sense of club identity at least insofar as the competition side was concerned. So with the Olympics out of the way and even though the 1985 World Championships were in view,

I was keen to start teaching on a regular basis rather than just go there to practise.

I have very definite views on the way judo should be taught and, as I mentioned earlier, I have been horrified by the standard of many of the young men now approaching national squad level. Most of the men, who come from clubs all over the country, may train three or four times a week, but the amount of learning they do during that time is minimal. It is only when you have had substantial training in the basics, such as uchi-komi, or studying the mechanics of basic throwing, that you can approach randori with a learning attitude. Most people I see doing randori are just having a good pull-around or desperately attempting not to lose face but there is no sense of study. Sometimes, it is good to go into a randori with a completely open mind and take what comes, but most of the time it is important to have a very clear idea of which techniques you think are likely to work against a particular opponent. All the time you should be noting what works and why and, just as important, what does not work and why. If you just come on the mat, have a practice and go off, without establishing one or two clear points that have emerged, it has been largely a waste of time or at least it has been if you are seriously hoping to improve.

Of course, it is part of the nature of judo that it brings together on one mat judoka with widely differing objectives. Some are aiming for the top of the competition ladder, some are trying to improve their skill, some are doing it as a hobby and yet some are there perhaps because they like fighting and at least doing it on a judo mat will keep them out of court. This confusion of purpose, when combined with the very wide variety of abilities and grades that you get on a judo mat, can cloud a sense of direction. But if you really want to learn, you have to study as well as sweat.

The reluctance to approach judo with any kind of academic attitude was brought home to me recently when I was invited by Roy Inman, manager of the Women's Squad, to give a talk to coaches from all over the country. All the county coaches and many of the club coaches were there and I was scheduled to give an hour's talk on the basics of coaching. I was about to start when I noticed that not one of them had a pad or a pencil. I told them I was astonished they had such amazing memories that they would be able to retain 60 minutes of information which even I found necessary to write down despite the fact that I had done all I was about to discuss. In the end, I refused to start until they had all fetched paper and pens to take notes, because I just wasn't going to waste my time and breath.

Unfortunately, I think the standard of judo teaching in the country is pretty abysmal and I believe we manage to produce men of international calibre in spite of the system rather than because of it. It is epitomised by the fact that in the area covered by Inner London Education Authority, it is possible to teach a class if you are a blue belt which I find unacceptable. No one should even consider teaching before first Dan, and that should be an absolute minimum. It is so easy to say that blue or brown belts can teach basics, but the so-called basics are often far more complex than people with that level of experience understand. Judo is a difficult and skilled sport, and if children or adults are started with suspect techniques, it is the worst possible foundation. The low standard of teaching applies right through the scale to country coach level so it is no wonder that some of the boys coming into the national squad cannot really throw anyone. In that sense, I was unbelievably lucky to have been able to study technicians, including not only Brian Jacks but also Dave Starbrook, whom I think is a very sound technician.

So I began teaching more regularly at the Budokwai towards the end of 1984 and have found it more rewarding than I imagined and certainly than I remembered from my early ILEA days. Teaching helps me to crystallise techniques or ideas that, after nearly 20 years of judo, are inseparable from my life on the mat. Over the next few years, I think there is going to be a change of emphasis in groundwork from armlocks to hold-downs and I am preparing the way for this in my classes. Sometimes, I will look at rolls or movements done by a host of champions from Sato, the Japanese team coach, to Takahashi, who had some simple but nifty ideas. There are times when I will teach my major techniques which I inevitably understand best of all, or change to a fairly obscure range of Russian sacrifice techniques which can work extremely well as a totally surprise move. At other times, I will try a different approach and work to get across the idea that judo is very much a game of strategy, where the object is not to batter away with one big gun in the hope that it will be successful, but that, by choosing a more oblique route, or disguising the entry, it is possible to use that 'big gun' even more effectively.

These few months as chief instructor at the Budokwai have given me a taste for teaching that I wasn't sure I had. Even though I stopped instructing regularly some years ago, I have, in the past two or three years, helped and encouraged the young boys in the national squad and I know that I have a lot to offer here and not only with the young boys either.

Judo has changed drastically in many ways since I began. For a start, it is becoming a truly international sport as can be seen from the result of the first Inter-Continental Championships held in Paris in February, 1984 (I was selected to fight, but had to withdraw through an elbow injury which is one of the very few that has prevented me from fighting) when a strong Asian team, dominated by the Japanese, was beaten by a European team fielding a number of second choices. It is now almost as worth while to go and study judo in France as to go to Japan though Japan remains the country with the greatest depth of top-quality players. Certainly, it is unquestionable that there is a European judo which has a distinct quality and the days when the Westerners would simply imitate the Japanese are over – or should be. For Westerners have different physiques, strengths and weaknesses and need to adapt their judo accordingly. Of course, we can still learn from the Japanese, particularly about style and gripping. The Japanese have always been very good at gripping, even though they are not big people with big muscles. Curiously, I have often found them extremely strong, but don't ask me where they get it from. Perhaps they really have an inner strength. I was fortunate in that I learnt a lot of my gripping from Jacks and supplemented it with a lot of hanging from bars and technically-sound gripping (gripping the jacket from under the sleeve on the seam), but my trips to Japan helped me to come to a broader understanding of grips.

There is also the more traditional side of judo, kata. I have, I must admit, done only one intensive weekend of kata in my whole judo career – and that was early in 1981 in preparation for my fourth Dan. Peter

The anxiety in my eyes says it all in the opening fight of the 1985 World Championships against Japan's Nobutoshi Hikage, which is not going as I had hoped

Donnelly and I spent two days doing nothing else but learning nage-no-kata, katame-no-kata and ju-no-kata and by the end we were becoming quite competitive about it. We had even thought of entering kata championships, but then the more conventional forms of championships intervened, and it was only when I started to think in terms of finalising my fifth Dan that I began to think of kata again. I had had my points for fifth Dan for two and a half years before I found the time to fulfil the kata requirement, which I suppose is an indication of my attitude towards grades and probably kata.

Competition has, without doubt, been more important to me than either grades or kata and while my main attention has been on the international contest mat, the former have been of lesser importance. But by the beginning of 1985, I felt I should finalise my fifth Dan, partly because the grade was expected of me by others, so once again I looked at the katas. I think now that it is important to keep the katas as part of the grading requirements (which is the only thing that will make most judoka do them) because it is part of judo's tradition. I don't think I learned anything by doing them, not at least from a technical point of view, and so long as it doesn't interfere with competition I don't think it does anyone any harm to learn them. And in the same way as when I am working with Ray on uchi-komi and it is going well, it gives a special kind of satisfaction, perhaps like two artists or dancers working well together.

Throughout the summer of 1985 I felt optimistic about the World Championships in Seoul in September because of my performance in the Europeans. Only one man, I felt, was likely to impede what I hoped would be a smooth return to World Champion status and that was Nobutoshi Hikage. But I had also heard reports from Japan that he hadn't really distinguished himself at all since the Moscow World Championships two years earlier.

My training with Ray Stevens had been going well and Alison and I had moved into a lovely garden flat near Crystal Palace. There were only a few ripples in my gradual build-up, which were caused by some organisational problems and these came to a head a month before we left for Asia when Colin McIver resigned as Director of Coaching and Training. He had experienced some difficulties working with the new triangular system within the British Judo Association where he oversaw the coaching work of Roy Inman and Arthur Mapp and, in addition, he finally decided he wanted to live in Scotland instead of moving to London. So when McIver became Technical Director for the Scottish Judo Association and Arthur Mapp was appointed team manager, I felt a little more responsibility for the team as a whole fell on my shoulders.

This did not interfere too much with our preparations, however, and it was an eager and confident team that left for Seoul. It was potentially one of the strongest teams Britain has ever sent to a World Championships with: Neil Eckersley (U60k); Stephen Gawthorpe (U65k); Kerrith Brown (U71k); me at U78k; Ray Stevens (U86k); Dennis Stewart (U95k); and Elvis Gordon at U95k and the Open. But there were two shocks waiting for us. Firstly, we had a horrendous journey when what should have been an uncomfortable 16 hours turned into a nightmare 44 hours of non-stop shuttling around to avoid various strikes. We arrived in Seoul shattered, and it took us four days to fully recover.

Then came the draw. It was the worst I had ever encountered in over a decade of international competition. Most of us had appalling draws which was just bad luck. Eckersley had Tamas Bujko, world silver medallist for his second fight, Gawthorpe had the Russian Sokolov for his first fight, Brown and Stevens were running into old adversaries and Stewart drew former Olympic Champion Van de Walle in the first round. I, however, suffered both from the amateur seeding system and an ironic twist of fate: my first fight was against none other than Nobutoshi Hikage himself. I couldn't believe it. For the two favourites (as we undoubtedly were) to meet in the first round made something of a mockery of the competition. And I knew I needed a couple of warm-up fights before I was ready to meet him.

It was a blow from which I never really recovered. The morning of 28 September 1985 – my twenty-seventh birthday – saw me go through my normal warm-up routine with Ray, who was also fighting that day, but I couldn't get going. I didn't feel paralysed by nerves, just rather dry and without spark or energy. I walked onto the mat – again wearing the white belt against Hikage's red, as in Moscow – only the fight turned out to be worse than Moscow. In 1983 I had attacked Hikage with all I had and could easily have won the decision. In Seoul, I could scarcely attack. Hikage repeated his strong push tactics, and I retreated. I just managed to avoid being thrown for a footsweep as I attempted to come forward, and from then only manged to put in the occasional attack. The matter was settled by a chui penalty which I was given for stepping off the fighting area.

Just how bad a mental state I was in was confirmed later in the day when I came back in the repechage, for though I beat Georgio Vismara (Italy), Kevin Docherty (Canada) and Waldemar Legien (Poland), I had to rely on decisions. I did not score a point all day, even though I had Legien's arm in my favourite armlock position. Of course, sport does not end with the final bell. As soon as I came off I had to face the Press. What had happened?

Was I going to retire? The French were as inquisitive as the English, though there were other reasons for that as I found out later when Jean-Luc Rouge, the French team manager, invited me to come to coach in France. I hedged by saying I was going to think it over for a month. In any case, there was still the rest of the championships to think about in which Stephen Gawthorpe, another 27-year-old incidentally, went on to win a bronze with superb groundwork.

It was only when I returned that I managed some sense of perspective on the whole affair. As John Goodbody – a sports journalist and former judo international himself whom I have known since I first came to the Budokwai – pointed out, I was the only competitor in Seoul who could claim four medals from four successive World Championships. In fact I was the only competitor with medals in every global event for the past eight years. And I had still won a bronze when far below my best. My decision not to retire wasn't just a case of pride or of not wanting to after such a depressing performance. I felt as if I had not finished the job to my satisfaction. That was all. All the offers of coaching abroad and other lucrative engagements were flattering – but they would have to wait. But I could not deny the fact that there was something amiss in my preparation. I have not lost two World and Olympic finals for technical reasons, yet it was difficult to pinpoint exactly what was going wrong. It was as if I kept making the same technical error, except that it wasn't as tangible as a bad attacking action.

The clues came from two of the friends I respect most. Other people may have said the same thing, but it was hearing these particular friends say it that actually made me take note – though I suppose I had always known it. Sitting in the Holmes Health Club before a practice one night, Jan Curtis, my best man, who had supported me through hours of conditioning training, said bluntly: 'You are doing too much conditioning and physical work and not enough judo. You are as fit and as strong as anyone else on the judo mat, Hikage included. Just go and do judo.' He pointed out how my run-up to the Norwegian Europeans had included the British Trials, the West German Open and the British Open, and then I had had a four-month lay-off before the World Championships. It was the advice my father had given me prior to Norway, and it had paid dividends. But I had forgotten it.

However, that was only part of the problem. The other one has not been so easy to solve. I have always respected Sharron's father, Terry, who is an extremely good coach; and it was Terry who really brought home to me yet again the one factor that has dogged my career since winning the World Championships in 1981. Shortly after coming home from Korea, he came to see Alison and me and said: 'It is is nothing physical . . . it is all up there,' pointing towards my head. And I know he is right though I still have not analysed which particular part of the psychological formula is missing. So long as imagination, motivation and determination can combine with technical excellence, the sportsman can organise his own life. But even those at the top of their sport will, on occasions, find themselves lacking in one or other, and this is where outside help in attaining the correct attitude is so crucial.

In India, I suppose they would call them gurus, in Japan senseis whereas in England we are happy with the word coach. Sportsmen and women in all fields have them though rarely do they retain links with the same person throughout their careers. I was one of the first in judo to have a personal coach when Cyril Carter started to advise me on my training. By the Moscow World Championships, however, our relationship had changed. While I was very grateful for all the help he had given me, I had outgrown him. Yet I had not managed to find anyone else whom I felt I could totally trust. The one exception was my father, and I now regret that he didn't continue to oversee my judo development when I came to London, though in another way, it was perhaps important that I was allowed to grow up away from him.

That kind of absolute trust between coach and athlete cannot be built up overnight, so I don't know what the future holds, but it is now clear that my psychological attitude is what I have to tackle next. I have no idea how long I will continue to compete, whether I will go on to the next World Championships in 1987, or even to the Seoul Olympics in 1988. All I know is that now is not the time to retire. I feel strongly that the Norwegian European Championships were not just an Indian summer and that the World Championships in Seoul were just a temporary setback. I have said all along that I will instinctively realise when it is the right time for me to retire and at this point – November 1985 – I am not even considering it. All I can hope is that as I move into my final years of competition, I will be able to enjoy them and get as much out of them in terms of the judo itself, and the international judo fraternity, as I have done in the past. Because in the final analysis, that is what judo is all about.

8

ACQUIRING THE BASIC SKILLS

The formidable complexity of judo technique makes it impossible to present a detailed analysis of my techniques within the scope of a book like this. Such an analysis would be more correctly the preserve of a specific handbook – or two. Nor was this the place for a consideration of the classical judo throws and groundwork which has already been covered extensively elsewhere. But what is rarely discussed is how the champions get to the top, the mistakes they make on the way and the strokes of fortune, or misfortune, that introduce them to the techniques with which they eventually conquer the world.

This is what I have tried to do in the ensuing chapters. It could almost be said to be an action replay of the first part of the book – but seen through an exclusively judo lens. I have looked back over the thousands of hours I have spent on the mat and considered which techniques were useful, which were a waste of time and which were positively harmful. I do discuss my techniques in some detail but really only to show how one man's judo develops and changes direction in response to the pressures of top competition, age and, of course, different personal influences. This, I hope, will be far more useful to teachers, aspiring champions and club players than a far-too-short examination of my uchi-mata or juji-gatame.

The Japanese are, by tradition, a very formal people and this seems to extend to most things they do and especially the way they teach and learn. They have a strict code of behaviour and sense of hierarchy and strongly believe in learning any subject step by step: it being necessary to master one step before moving on to another. This, I think, is the great strength of the Japanese system but also its great weakness. It is a strength because the stages of progress are clearly marked but it is a weakness because the system can become so rigid that it will not adapt to new demands. And this can be seen in the way judo is taught. There is no doubt that judo has flourished throughout the world partly because it offers a structured and safe system for satisfying one of the basic instincts of mankind – fighting – in a manner which makes for a totally absorbing study. When you think about the possibilities of injury from huge and forceful throws, strangles and armlocks, it is surprising how relatively free from injury judo remains.

The major reason for this, of course, are the different types of breakfalls which form the introduction to judo in most clubs throughout the world and my early clubs in Rugby and Coventry were no exception. I went through what appeared to me to be the laborious routine of side, rear, and rolling breakfalls as all children and adults do. At first they were quite fun but gradually I began to find them boring and for quite a long period I thought they were a waste of time, even when my father imaginatively tried to vary them with gymnastic tumbling routines and cartwheels. I just wanted to get on with my judo. Although I didn't realise it, there was a fashion in Britain for a time to regard breakfalls as a hindrance to judo. By practising how to fall, the argument went, you were teaching yourself how to be thrown, whereas you should be concentrating on learning all the ways possible not to be thrown. Fortunately, my father didn't agree and even now, when taking a class, I will lead a breakfall routine at the start.

I am now convinced that, when practising randori, if you know you can breakfall correctly, you have the confidence to experiment and to take risks in order to expand your judo skills. If on the other hand, you are not happy with being thrown because each time you get slightly bumped or bruised, and it becomes a painful experience, then you will be stiff and defensive in practice and so busy stopping yourself being thrown that you won't learn to throw others well. In short, having inadequate breakfalls limits your ability to learn on the mat.

The best judoka to prove this point are the Japanese. Not only do they breakfall, and do it well, but you can see that they are confident enough to learn while being thrown. In Japan, there is a totally different attitude towards being thrown from that which exists in this country. The British, and especially the top competitors, don't like going over because they feel that even in training, they have reputations to maintain. If a member of the British squad gets bowled over, you can see him get up hurriedly and glance around to see if anyone witnessed the 'disgrace'. From the fuss some people make, you would think it was a national incident if I am thrown in the Budokwai on a Tuesday practice night. But in Japan, everyone gets thrown. During the last practice before the 1984 Olympics, in a small dojo in the Japanese area of Los Angeles, Yamashita, eight times All-Japan Champion, was thrown with a cracking ouchi-gari by one of his junior training partners, and the champion's immediate reaction was to congratulate his partner with a friendly cuff across the head. Then he threw him with two wonderful throws just to reassert his rightful superiority. The other disadvantage of spending a whole evening's randori trying not to be thrown is that there is a real danger of injury as you try to twist out of the throw. Most of the time it is simply not worth it.

I can't remember being taught my first throws but the first one I really took to was morote-seoi-nage. I don't know how it came about, and though I must have been taught the throw at one stage, I don't remember learning it. As far as I know, it came completely naturally to me. It was a very high technique – I have never done a dropping seoi-nage to the right. I stood upright, took a good grip on my opponent and then moved around a lot. When it felt 'right', I wrapped my right arm in the jacket, made the connection and launched my opponent. I know that that description is not much use to anyone trying to learn the technique, but I can't describe it in very much more detail which is one of the difficulties of a technique that comes naturally to you. It is very different with my tai-otoshi which I learnt painstakingly. One important point I do remember about learning morote-seoi-nage: the success of the throw depended on the speed of the upright spin, which, in turn, increased the speed of the throw. It is a bit like when ice skaters do turns, twists or spins and tuck in their elbows so that they go around very quickly. If their elbows are jutting out, they are slowed down. The principle, I think, is to spin very tightly.

Morote-seoi-nage is one of the first throws that is taught to children and so it is very popular among small kids. Another reason for its popularity is that it is much easier for a small child to throw a bigger opponent with it than, say with tai-otoshi or uchi-mata, because they can just wrap in tightly. My problem, and I think the problem of many children, was that I did only morote-seoi-nage. I used it far too much and was always looking to throw with it. I would occasionally use ouchi-gari to try to open my opponent up a bit if I was having real difficulties because he was crouching so low that his bottom was only six inches off the ground in defence. I also remember my father telling me to do uchi-komi on ouchi-gari and particularly the variation where my right hand quickly slides my partner's jacket off his left shoulder to bring him down onto the leg I want to reap. That used to work quite well. But I really wanted to launch opponents with seoi-nage because it was so spectacular. Eventually, however, my opponents became used to it, and even though I could enter it from any angle, I began to be dragged back more and more often. I was also getting bigger, so perhaps I was slightly losing my co-ordination for that particular throw. Maybe it just needed rethinking and readjusting, but my injury stopped me using it anyway. My groundwork, meanwhile, was not bad. Like all kids, I did kesa-gatame because it is one of the first holds you are taught but I also did kame-shiho-gatame and a kind of mune-gatame. But, at this stage, I wasn't really interested in groundwork.

From the time I started judo at seven to my teens, I relied on my one big throw and though I thought I was training hard and well, I wasn't really. I did a bit of uchi-komi but all my entries into the throws, the timings and the groundwork moves developed naturally in the randori sessions which I enjoyed most of all. I think that if someone had watched for my weaknesses and my strong points, I could have widened my scope a lot more at an earlier age and perhaps avoided injury. My father was able to help slightly, but he was only a brown belt then and later a first Dan, so his experience was limited. But apart from my over-reliance on one throw, I know that my father and the instructors at Coventry gave me a good start.

Of course, there are things that both my father and I would do differently now with the benefit of nearly 20 years' intensive judo. First of all, I think judo up to teenage level should primarily be fun. Until that age, you are learning basics and it needs to be purely enjoyable. When I trained my dog Bob as a puppy, I always gave him a reward and children are the same in that they need to be encouraged; it is no good punishing children if they get a technique wrong.

I think I would teach a limited number of throwing techniques rather than confuse beginners with a vast range so that they can do none of them well. With just four or so techniques they can learn principles which can then be applied with greater ease to other techniques. For instance, if a boy is defending and is difficult to throw forwards, then perhaps he is susceptible to a rear throw, or he is better at defending to one side and is weak on the other. Eliminating potential weakpoints is more important, I think, than teaching 15 different standing techniques.

One of judo's great advantages is its immense variety of techniques but this does raise a problem when it comes to teaching beginners. Many of the techniques are equally difficult, so which ones should be taught first? I would select one of the seoi-nages – probably morote because it teaches you to use your hands; and I would probably choose tai-otoshi as well. I think it is important, also, to introduce a throw off one leg. Rather than osoto-gari, I would probably pick ouchi- or kouchi-gari, which would teach them to think right from the start. I remember I consistently used to practise the four reaping throws, osoto-gari and kosoto-gari, ouchi-gari and kouchi-gari, and I am still using all four to good effect today.

I would also teach ogoshi as a basic throw. My father practised a lot of ogoshi with me, from quite early on, and the firm hold around my partner's waist taught me how important hip contact was. Looking back, I think that my success with morote-seoi-nage was based on this feeling for close hip contact that was developed through ogoshi and which certainly played an important role in the development of my tai-otoshi.

On the ground, I always teach basic principles rather than specific holds. I think it is better to tell beginners, regardless of whether they are children or adults, that there are thousands of holds you can get your partner into as long as you apply the basic rules. These are: (a) don't get your legs tangled up with your partner's and (b) control your partner's head and one of his arms. That's all they need to know at that stage. This way you avoid the problem of kids going for kesa-gatame on the right and going all round the body to get to it because that is how they have been taught. Only when beginners have grasped these basic principles, is it time to introduce more techniques.

On a more general point, it is worth pointing out to beginners that judo is about controlling your opponent and though throws tend to work more by accident than design when you are inexperienced, certain principles must be observed for techniques (throws or holds) to work. These are: (a) body contact; (b) head control; (c) correct positioning of your body to operate the chosen technique; (d) direction of throw/position of hold; and (e) speed of execution.

It is important to say again here how lucky I was to have parents who limited my competitive activity. There are too many children entering too many competitions and I have come across cases where they are competing every Saturday and sometimes on Sundays as well. I call them 'pot hunters' because they are just seeing how many pots they can win. It is very sad, particularly because they are not really improving and in the end, more often than not, the child doesn't make it into senior judo. Nine times out of ten, a 'pot-hunting' child has an ambitious parent behind him who just doesn't realise the damage he is causing. They may not be killing their children but they are certainly killing any enjoyment they might get from the sport. Up to teenage level and even beyond, there is no reason to take part in more than a dozen competitions a year. One a month is more than enough and immeasurably better than one a week or more.

The back injury I gained from getting pulled back in morote-seoi-nage forced me to learn tai-otoshi but during the long and frustrating transitional period, I relied heavily on ouchi-gari and, later, kouchi-gari. It was fortunate that my father had started me on ouchi-gari when I was very young. He used to look at a technique very objectively and study it in as much detail as he could and then we would work on it; and this is what happened with the arm-over variation of ouchi-gari. I hold my partner's left lapel with my right hand and stand with my right leg extended behind me. I then swing my right arm over my opponent's left shoulder and place my right leg between his legs very deep so that I am fully committed for the reaping action. We worked on that for a long time and at one Espoir Championships I won every match with it. I can still use it and scored a good one in the 1981 World Championships.

Gradually my tai-otoshi started to work. One of the difficulties of judo is that people follow the textbook ideal too closely without adapting the technique to suit their individual physiques. I had to find a tai-otoshi which was right for me and that took time. I know that mine is not theoretically correct, but it works for me.

Dave Starbrook's famous tai-otoshi relied heavily on the strength of his upper body but there was no point in my trying to model myself on him because my body is totally different. Although I can never match Starbrook's strength, I am reasonably supple. So, I favour a much wider split of the legs which has the advantage of dropping me much lower in relation to my opponent and thus well below his centre of gravity. But to be able to do this, I found it essential to open up my opponent and get inside the reach of his arms and I learned to do this from an orthodox right-handed grip. I then pull sharply upwards and outwards with both hands, exactly at the point when I start to turn in for the throw, thus ensuring firm body contact. When done at speed, it ensures the loss of my opponent's balance and the perfect body position from which to complete the technique. I found that my right hip shouldn't go past my partner's right hip but that it should have contact with it. My right leg then snakes over and traps my opponent's right leg. I then transfer some weight onto that right leg but, unusually perhaps, most of my weight remains on my left leg. Since those early days, I have added a little extra 'finish'. As I pull my opponent's right sleeve to finish off the throw, I straighten my right leg to give my opponent a little lift to bring him up and over. It may not sound or look like the classical tai-otoshi but with occasional adjustments and additions, it has served me well over many years.

Like my morote-seoi-nage, my early successes with tai-otoshi came not only from the hours of practice – and I did work extremely hard to perfect it – but also from the speed of attack. At this stage, I didn't really think about when I made the entry but relied on speed and a developing 'instinct' for the right time to attack. After a year or so of struggling to throw anyone with it, you can imagine my sense of relief and achievement when it started to work.

Most of my judo at this time used the orthodox right-handed grip. My morote-seoi-nage and tai-otoshi came from this grip and I would change it only for the arm-over ouchi-gari. I don't think that gripping is important at the junior stage and consider there is too much emphasis at the moment on teaching kids to change and fight for grips. So many contests just end up with the kids pulling each other's jackets around and failing to carry out one positive technique. I don't agree with many Japanese views on the teaching of judo apart from their attitude towards, as I said earlier,

From tai-otoshi to armlock textbook style, except that this took place in the early rounds of the 1981 European Championships in Hungary against Jacobsen (Denmark). Using the cross-grip, I turned Jacobsen over his right foot, whipped him into the air, put him on his back and immediately swung round for juji-gatame

breakfalls and grips. The teach good, basic grips from which kids must learn to operate their major techniques. Only later should more complex gripping skills be introduced.

Much the same applies at this age to fitness. Up to the early teens, kids can do a little running if they want – most of them run around anyway and have quite a high level of natural stamina – and they need only take running a little more seriously by 14 or 15. Suppling is very important and can be done at any age. It is important to keep the muscles stretched, particularly if they are doing quite a lot of judo, which tends to constrict rather than to extend muscles. But apart from their judo training and the general sports they do at school I don't think there is any need for extra fitness training until they reach their mid-teens. I certainly don't think there is any need for weight training until 16 or so though it depends on body size and some lads are quite big for their age. However, too many youngsters are starting on weights too early and without really knowing what they are doing. So, unless they have access to very good instruction, I would suggest they keep off weights until 16 or so.

The same age limit should apply to armlocks and strangles because the danger of injury is too great. It is so easy to injure someone badly or to frighten a young child. In any case, I don't think that waiting until 16 does anyone any harm, though exceptions could be made for particularly advanced children. This means that youngsters have to build a firm groundwork foundation on hold-downs, which is not a bad thing at all, rather than dive for the more spectacular but more elusive armlocks and strangles.

Similar rules of basic common sense apply to dieting or dehydrating to make a weight category – again, it is just not worth it – or to training or even competing through injury. You have to ask what are children doing judo for? In the end, safety must be paramount. After all, they are just children and medals, titles and other achievements must be seen in perspective. Up to the age of 15 or 16, youngsters need to be given a reliable, sensible foundation in technique which will allow them to make the transition to senior level safely and to maintain a fresh and positive attitude that has not been destroyed by 'pot hunting'. I will also make them eager to widen their judo skills and the most ambitious will be keen to start aiming for the senior national squad.

9

THE PATH TO THE WORLD TITLE

As I said earlier, I left Coventry in 1974 because it was obvious both to my father and to members of Coventry Judo Club, notably Brian Perryman, that I needed the involvement with the international judo scene of London in order to progress. Just like all careers, it is important to know when to move on; it became very clear on arriving in London that I was on the bottom rung of a new ladder but at least I was firmly on it. There were all the incidental problems of learning to survive on the Budokwai mat and how not to be strangled out by Brian Jacks but these were incidental to the main lesson. I had to learn how to study.

Up to then, I had been advised, encouraged, rewarded and punished as I learned, but a change of attitude had become essential. I learnt that it is necessary to think about judo, to watch others extremely carefully and to watch oneself. It became clear that it is not enough to go on the mat just to work up a good sweat but that there has to be a purpose to the training. From the countless possibilities of a randori session, certain basic patterns of movement have to emerge, patterns that can be recognised and repeated. Within the whirl of improvisation in a fast attack, counter, attack again, there has to be some methodical process so that when the problem occurs again, the solution is instantly at hand. There is not enough time in the short span of a competitive career to rely purely on instinct and experience; methodical study is crucial.

Little of this occurred to me so clearly in 1975; it was something that took shape over the years. In fact the system that I now follow, which includes periods of specific conditioning training, revision and development of new techniques all programmed to bring me to a peak just before a competition, evolved in a far more haphazard manner than the way I am going to describe it.

The point was that even in the mid-1970s, judo training still largely followed the Japanese traditions which upheld the ideal of hard and uncompromising sessions where the main lessons were learned in the heat of the randori practice. Most of the fitness work, suppling work, development of new techniques and uchi-komi were all squeezed into the 90-minute or 2-hour evening practice. Underlying all was the basic premise that to do judo well in competition, the best preparation was judo and more judo. And beneath that, for some, was the even more traditional attitude that judo was shugyo or an ascetic character training, meaning that you really learned through hardship only.

However, I didn't fall into either the 'good sweat' category or the 'prove yourself or die' category. I wanted to improve my judo skills in order to win competitions as quickly and efficiently as possible and I felt more in tune with Western sportsmen in other fields such as athletics and gymnastics than with any specific Japanese traditions. This even extended to the lack of tradition within judo of a personal coach, which is a standard feature in most other sports on the Olympic calendar. So I was extremely lucky to meet Cyril Carter.

Until 1975 I was quite happy to allow judo practice alone to improve my strength, endurance and suppleness but I was soon to learn that there were faster and more efficient methods for producing such changes, based on sound principles of sports science that have been established through research in other sports. Success in sport depends quite simply on producing the correct blend and achieving the highest level of ability in what are called the five Ss: Skill, Speed, Stamina, Strength and Suppleness (with a sixth 'S' for Psychology). Skill is the elimination of any difference between the intention and execution of a technique. Speed is a mixture of two factors: the time taken for each individual muscle to contract and the co-ordination of such contractions in all muscle groups when performing a particularly complex movement. The potential of the first is determined at birth and is unalterable, while the second is capable of improvement through suitable training.

Stamina refers to the efficiency of the heart and lungs in supplying oxygen to the working muscles (cardio-vascular endurance). Strength is divided into local endurance (the ability to repeat movements continuously while carrying a fixed load) and power (the ability to exert maximum force against resistance). Finally, Suppleness, probably one of the most neglected areas of training, seeks to improve a player's ability to extend his major joints to their maximum range without risk of injury.

From Cyril, I learned how important it is to work at these areas in order to provide the optimum physiological basis for top-level judo. To these qualities would later be added other refinements such as: triple-phasing (the idea of dividing training programmes into phases concentrating on endurance, power and speed); overcoming plateaus in learning and achievement (those well-known periods when you just can't seem to improve); peaking (hitting top form at the right time); kinaesthesis (body awareness or feedback); and many others which may have been absent in traditional Japanese practice but which are part and parcel of modern day sport.

Cyril was working with Brian Jacks when I first met him, so he was aware how much judo training resided in the Dark Ages in comparison with preparation for athletics or rowing. But he had had experience with judo players and without hesitation made me start my training diary and set me my first training programme. This consisted of: a fundamental suppling routine every day; a local endurance strength circuit alternating with a strength-in-extension programme every 48 hours; and alternating a shuttle-running routine with extended two to three mile runs to improve my heart and lungs. All this plus judo five times a week.

From this fairly simple routine grew far more sophisticated programmes designed to combat specific difficulties I was encountering on the mat or to give me the physical base from which to perform tasks against particular opponents or to bring me to a peak at a certain point. Looking back, this seems such an obvious development that I am still surprised that it took so long for such preparation training to be introduced to judo; and I am even more surprised that so many aspiring contest judo players still pursue relatively crude preparation programmes.

This preparation proved crucial to my success in judo but at the time it seemed an added bonus to the real training I did in the evening at the Budokwai. The charisma of Brian Jacks and the spectacular features of his uchi-mata inevitably had its effect and I began working on the throw myself. The basic throw did not present any major difficulties for me, because again, the ogoshi that I had done from a very early age was the perfect preparation. But the entry required special study. There are two main methods of entering the uchi-mata: the 'spinning' and what I call the 'catch-up'. The spinning method was Brian Jacks's superb master weapon with which he achieved some dramatic results, particularly when combining a spinning left uchi-mata with a right tai-otoshi. It was also the first entry into the technique I learnt.

Taking an orthodox right grip (though I have since learned to do it using a variety of grips), I first move my opponent to my left. Keeping my weight firmly on my left leg and with my right leg extended behind me, I pivot on the ball of my left foot and simultaneously swing my right leg around and across my opponent's body. As I execute the turn, I hop towards my opponent on my left leg to achieve the firm contact between my back and the front of his right hip. At the point of contact, my right leg sweeps upwards against my opponent's left thigh and I complete the technique by launching my upper body forward while my right leg continues a positive upward sweeping action.

It is important to keep this sweeping right leg completely straight (obviously the more supple player is at a distinct advantage when executing this technique). The sweeping right leg and back should operate very much like a see-saw, so that when your chest goes down your leg goes up. If the player loses any tension in his hips in the uchi-mata, the attack becomes very weak and easy to escape from.

As with all my standing techniques, I strongly favour adopting an upright posture in order to execute the uchi-mata with as straight a back as possible. This style of fighting has two distinct advantages: firstly, a straight back is anatomically correct and therefore the risk of injury smaller and secondly a straight back acts as a strong and efficient lever when executing any throw and no matter in which direction that throw is to be made. Unfortunately, many players feel 'weak' when they adopt an upright stance because they have become accustomed to defending from a crouching position. But though they may feel safer when bent over, the position limits their attacking capabilities.

The static or 'catch-up' uchi-mata is predominantly a Japanese technique though the French often use it for it favours their strong one-sided stance: they always have their right or left foot placed prominently forward. I first saw Sonoda and Nose use it in Japan and after watching the French, I began to work on it myself because I knew it would be a worth-while addition to the spinning method – if one didn't work, the other probably would. The technique is generally used when both players are standing relatively still. I start by ensuring that my left leg is in an off-square position and then advance my right foot to a point between my opponent's legs in order to achieve hip contact. My right foot is in contact with the ground for a moment only while my left foot 'catches up' to replace it at that point so that my right leg can continue the sweeping action. The completion of the technique is exactly the same as for the spinning uchi-mata. It is worth noting here that the French, particularly, have incorporated an ouchi-gari lead-in for the 'catch-up' uchi-mata, actually hooking for an ouchi-gari, but then changing to a swift and at times devastating uchi-mata.

Uchi-mata remains one of the top scoring techniques in major competitions which shows how important a throw it is. But it isn't easy to do well because it demands complex co-ordination and the ability to work well on one leg. It was about two years after starting to work on it that I started to throw with it in international competition, proving that perseverance is necessary.

Throughout those first years at the Budokwai, while working away at the uchi-mata, I was improving and extending my tai-otoshi. The specific work I was doing on the strength-in-extension programme was having a dramatic effect on my left-hand pull and on my ability to execute an extremely low tai-otoshi and yet to retain the spring in my legs to come up suddenly. I noticed how much my pull improved because opponents would find themselves stepping over my leg but still reeling onto their backs because of the force from it.

However, I had learnt from my morote-seoi-nage days that it was no good just concentrating on one throw and I looked at possible combinations. Kouchi-gari linked perfectly with tai-otoshi because the initial body movement is identical, thus making it extremely difficult if not impossible for my opponent to judge which throw I am going to use: is he about to be thrown forwards or backwards? When I linked these two throws, I concentrated particularly on the firm contact between my right forearm and my opponent's chest to be able to drive him towards his rear right-hand corner which is the perfect break-of-balance for kouchi-gari.

Obviously, with a combination technique like this, the throw I use in the end depends entirely on my opponent's reaction. So, if my opponent reacts to the initial movement by attempting to resist a tai-otoshi attack by swiftly shifting his weight onto his right foot, then that will be my cue to

---

My wide-split tai-otoshi – made possible by doing regular suppling – bringing me another ippon, this time in the British open in 1985

switch to kouchi-gari. If he does not react swiftly enough, or fails to react at all, then the initial movement can carry through to execute tai-otoshi. The timing and judgement so vital to combination techniques is virtually impossible to teach and, as in boxing where a fighter must read the movements of his opponent to judge from which direction the next blow will come, so it is very much a matter of speed of thought, reflexes and considerable experience whether you press home the first attack or change to the second throw. In the end, you don't think about it, you just do it.

New techniques take time to be assimilated. Sometimes, it takes a couple of years to absorb a new throw, and the same is true of combination techniques. I may have had quite a good tai-otoshi by 1975–76 and started to develop quite a good uchi-mata by 1976–77, but it was not until 1978 that I began putting the two throws together, after I had instinctively used them to great effect by throwing Nishida flat on his back in the Kano Cup. I had attacked with tai-otoshi a couple of times and he had casually stepped over. Without thinking, on the third entry I switched to an uchi-mata and Nishida was caught. I had accidentally discovered another combination worth studying.

My wide-split tai-otoshi seen from another angle, against Gunther Kruger in the 1979 European Championships, Brussels

The mentally stimulating aspect of judo techniques can be seen from my next development. As my uchi-mata and tai-otoshi became stronger, I began to encounter rigid defences based on a firm, not to say nearly straight, left arm. My answer, after some study, was the standing armlock. First of all, I create space between my opponent and myself by quickly moving away from him and simultaneously removing my right hand from his lapel. By circling my right arm over the top of my opponent's straight left arm and continuing the circling movement around and under his arm, I start to execute a locking action on his elbow. Swiftly removing my left hand from my opponent's sleeve, I place it above his left elbow and it can be relatively simple to gain a submission or to take him down into groundwork.

As the 1980 Moscow Olympics approached, my judo was slowly taking a distinctive shape and as new techniques were added to the repertoire, they were carefully dovetailed into the existing favourites so that everything linked together like a jigsaw. From my uchi-mata I could go into tai-otoshi and from tai-otoshi I could go into kouchi-gari; from kouchi-gari into a standing armlock to clear an oppenent's stiff arm – which then allowed me in for the uchi-mata again. Of course, I had other techniques, such as my ouchi-gari and osoto-gari which would all come out in a moment's notice. But they were all done on the right-hand side which is perhaps curious because I am naturally left-handed. However, for some time I had had one left-handed technique that I knew I could rely on under pressure and particularly when fighting awkward, left-handed players: ippon-seoi-nage.

The major advantage of this throw is that it is done with only one hand gripping the opponent's judogi. When executing my uchi-komi, I have always practised the throw from a standing position, turning in left, locking in tight with my left arm and establishing good hip contact. But with scarcely a thought in contest, I whip in for drop left ippon-seoi-nage and through the years I have scored some thundering ippons with it including a beauty against Fratica of Romania in Moscow in 1983 when the whole stadium echoed with the bang as he hit the deck. But it is a throw I rarely use in randori and almost never as a dropping throw, so it really is something that just comes out of the blue. Not all my throws have been the result of methodical study. There is still room, and must always be room, for a burst of spontaneity.

One of the legacies from my junior days which I clung to for a considerable time after I moved to London was a marked preference for throwing rather than for groundwork. My groundwork wasn't bad, as can be seen from the fact that I have never been either held-down or

My left drop seoi-nage is probably my fastest technique and has brought me a string of successes throughout my career. Here is an early example against Gunther Kruger in the 1979 European Championships, Brussels

armlocked in contest which is not a bad record for a top competitive career spanning nearly two decades. So perhaps that was why my only groundwork defeat, Gilbert's strangle in the British Open in 1978, had such a profound effect on me. Although I had never been caught before, I didn't brush it off as a once-in-a-lifetime fluke and I certainly wasn't going to get caught again. I have said that one of my strongest assets, in addition to a certain natural ability, is a capacity to learn quickly from mistakes. If I had dismissed that loss to Gilbert as a minor slip I would never have won the World Championship title. It threw a revealing spotlight onto my understanding of groundwork and it was obvious that I didn't know enough. So I set out to do something about it.

It was apparent from the beginning of my groundwork study that I didn't have the clear, set patterns and precise understanding of intricate moves and linking techniques that I was developing in my standing work. I had a fair repertoire of turns and I was fairly competent in the three areas of holding, armlocks and strangles. But I relied on speed, strength and an innate tumbling ability to put my partner between my legs at moments of stress or to enable me to come out securely on top in the more unclear tussles.

I knew that I had to do far more methodical uchi-komi practice on the ground, look at the most frequent situations that occur and learn to produce instant answers. So much groundwork that could be seen then (and still can be seen in the 1980s) was so inconclusive and unclear because no one had taken the trouble to make a formal study of it. Yet, in many ways, it is easier to become extremely good at groundwork than it is to become adept at standing work. Throwing depends partly on study and partly on speed, reflexes and the flamboyant risk taking that is really the preserve of youth. Groundwork, on the other hand, is more like a game of chess. There is time to look for weaknesses in your opponent and to decide what to do. You can sometimes afford to let your opponent clearly see a groundwork attack to make him defend and open himself to attack elsewhere. You can afford to develop lines of attack on the ground, gradually securing one arm, then moving towards another; controlling the head and slowly but surely drawing your partner onto his back and into a vice-like hold. Speed has its place on the ground but control is far more crucial.

However, I had to decide on a definite pattern or area of work and that didn't come overnight. I tried various slick moves I had seen or half-developed during my contest career, but for some time after my defeat by Gilbert I hadn't come to a firm decision. Then later that year I saw Iastkevich, the Russian U86k fighter at the 1978 European Championships again, and I was impressed by the decisiveness of his armlock routine. The Russians had, I knew, spent 15 years working on juji-gatame, and sometimes you see ridiculous matches where Russian fighters move all over the place on the ground, ignoring a hundred and one opportunities for holds or strangles, just to get their armlocks. But such singlemindedness does pay dividends, for at the very least it takes the indecision out of judo: if you do only one move but do it well, it is better than a dozen mediocre ones. Apart from all this, I had a certain temperamental affinity with armlocks. Having favoured a standing armlock, the transition to working on that elbow joint on the ground was a natural one, and not least because I saw it as the quickest way, apart from throwing, of achieving the goal of judo – ippon.

I had watched Iastkevich carefully at the European Championships, but not carefully enough as I realised much later. I went home and began studying the various ways of turning an opponent from the standard defensive position of all fours into the armlock. Iastkevich worked mainly on the right, but I felt more natural working on the left. Attacking from the rear right-hand corner, I hook my left arm through my opponent's left arm, simultaneously straddling his back and hooking my left foot behind and under his left knee. With my left arm under my opponent's left armpit, I grip his wrist. Still firmly gripping my opponent's left wrist, I drop my

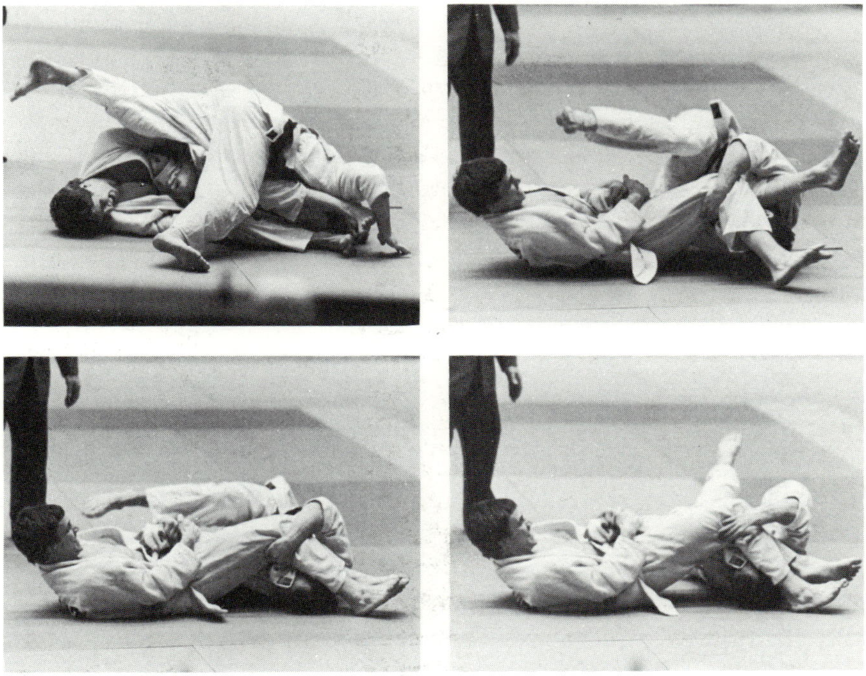

The basic form of my armlock roll seen in operation against Gunther Kruger at the 1979 World Championships, Paris

right shoulder onto the floor while at the same time slipping my right leg around and underneath his chin. As I start to pull hard on my opponent's left arm, I then straighten my left leg under his body while lifting his head with my right leg in order to force him into turning over onto his back.

Once in the classical armlock position, I bring my right arm under his left forearm and start to pull his wrist up in the direction of his head where he is weakest. However, the angle must not be sufficiently acute to allow him the opportunity to bridge out.

I thought that that was the technique used by Iastkevich but when I went back and studied some videos of him in action, I saw that his technique was slightly different in that he puts his leg on the back of his opponent's neck and reaches round with his hand to pick up his opponent's near leg and pull him round and over. So, like my tai-otoshi, my hours of work produced not a classical move nor a perfect copy of an existing technique, but something new. And I didn't stop there. I learned to improve my roll by putting a half nelson on my opponent's left arm which gave me much more leverage, and I learned to do it on the right as well as the left.

I also taught myself to link it with the most basic armlock roll of all. This is where, picking up my opponent's left arm again from a back-straddle position, and slipping my right leg under my opponent's chin, I put my left shoulder to the ground and flip my opponent over onto his back. I also learned Iastkevich's roll, so that after a year or so, I began to be quite competent at turning judoka from an all-fours position, changing from one technique to another, according to the reactions of my opponent.

As the Moscow Olympics drew nearer, my groundwork became increasingly secure. In addition to the armlock moves, I had studied the most fundamental strangle of all, hadaka-jime, partly because it could be entered from the same basic position I used for juji-gatame and partly because it allowed me to use the strength of my forearms to secure a firm grip. I straddle my opponent's back while simultaneously hooking both my feet under his thighs and slipping both my arms under his armpits to grip his wrists. By extending my arms and legs at the same time, I flatten my opponent on the ground; I maintain the lifting and straightening action of my feet and legs to prevent him using his lower body and legs as a means of escape. I then slide my left arm under his throat so that the inner edge of my forearm is pressed against his Adam's apple and secure a grip with my right hand in my left. By pressing down on the back of his head with my shoulder and at the same time pulling with my right hand, the strangle is now in operation and a submission obtainable. With the strangle and the armlock both becoming known at international as well as domestic level, I was able to move from one to another and my opponents really didn't know what was coming.

Between 1975 and 1981, the shape of my adult judo was formed. It took a combination of formal study, personal observation, encouragement from friends, advice from senior judo men, luck and the occasional Gilbert-like shock, but I served my apprenticeship and, on the whole, used the time well. However, I did things then that are simply not appropriate now. For instance, with all the optimism, drive and hunger of youth, I worked through injuries and illnesses in a way that now horrifies me, but in a sense, it was a positive mistake. I became accustomed to setting both long- and short-term goals and working clearly towards them, though for much of that time there was no question of following the kind of sophisticated peaking programme that I now adhere to. I had an apprenticeship to serve, and that meant entering competitions at least once every five weeks or so, which makes it impossible to think in terms of peaking. But contest for me, even at this stage, was not just a tilt at a medal, but part of the learning process and after each event I would note what had worked and what had not.

Developing parallel with my technical ability was, I hoped, a more sophisticated psychological attitude to judo. For years, I had not known what it was like to live a normal life, for behind everything I did lay another imminent competition. It may have been a small domestic competition or a major international, but I could never completely relax. Each time I sat in a cinema with Helen or went out for a meal with friends, my mind would stray to the next event, or to a judo problem which I had yet to resolve. It is as much part of judo training to come to terms with this mental pressure as with the feeling of an opponent's strong hands gripping your jacket. And though I presented a friendly and confident exterior, the pressure did tell. Often, it was only noticeable by a certain arrogance and only my close friends could see through it. Pressure, disappointment and success are all part and parcel of technical obstacles that have to be overcome in any sport, including judo. Looking back at that time, perhaps I made more mental errors than technical ones because there is no doubt in my mind that I was technically proficient enough to have won one Olympic title and one World title by 1980. But coping with the mental aspects of judo is as important as natural talent or hard work and the fact that I didn't win those titles showed that however well I had dealt with the technical obstacles, answers to some of the psychological difficulties had not been so readily forthcoming.

As 1980 changed into 1981, I added little that was new to my repertoire, but concentrated on improving my existing techniques and making them work more naturally in practice. I felt comfortable applying tai-otoshi from a number of grips, including the cross-grip, where my right hand grasps my opponent's right collar. The rules forbid you to hold both sides of your partner's jacket unless you are making an attack, so I couldn't walk around gripping them. But the cross-grip was useful when I was still trying to get a good grip on my opponent's right sleeve and the one-sided grip (using both hands) did produce some devastating tai-otoshis.

It was, however, becoming a little more difficult to manoeuvre my opponents into a position from which I could use my main techniques because they were becoming so well-known. So I had to develop a larger repertoire of small, opening techniques and one of these, a kouchi-gari, came from the cross-grip. I was finding extremely defensive left-handed players a particular problem and this proved to be one answer especially when they were preventing me from getting a grip on their right sleeves. As my opponent pulls his arm away, I quickly move my left foot to his extreme right, forcing his weight onto his right leg by pushing firmly with my right hand, either against his chest if I have a cross-grip or by controlling his head if I have an orthodox right-collar grip. With a rapid hooking and reaping action, I then drive my opponent sharply backwards. It needs an exaggerated, bold movement but it is a movement that is still with me and which I still do with considerable success.

Another important opener which came into play about this time was the kosoto-gari used specifically against left-handers. The extreme left-hander usually adopts an off-square stance with his left leg placed forward which makes it impossible for me to use my strongest techniques, so I had to find a way of making such an opponent step back onto his left leg. The only way to force him do this is to attack his left leg and this is where kosoto-gari came in. In the same way that Dave Starbrook used to employ a kosoto-gake with tai-otoshi, I press home a strong attack with kosoto-gari and, just as my opponent alters his body alignment by withdrawing his left leg, I swing my right leg across for tai-otoshi. The one key to this combination is speed and I have been known, on occasions, to start with kosoto-gari, move into tai-otoshi and at the last moment, switch the whole attack to uchi-mata (but so fast that it has to be instinctive, because there is no time to think). There have been times when the experienced left-hander has preferred to risk a lower score with kosoto-gari and has almost refused to move his left leg sufficiently far for me to attack with tai-otoshi. However, as my groundwork became stronger, either option became suitable for my purposes!

Another useful combination against the stubborn left-hander was right osoto-gari into left ippon-seoi-nage. I had always used these throws individually but the time had come to firmly link them together into a perfect combination. As I have already pointed out, the extreme left-hander stands off-square to the right with his supporting right leg extended behind him. Quite often, I would attack my opponent with ostoto-gari only to find that I couldn't throw him because he had transferred his weight onto his left leg. When this happened, I found it quite easy to encourage him to transfer his weight by faking osoto-gari with my hands and, at the last moment, removing my left hand and whipping smartly into a drop left ippon-seoi-nage, which at this time must have been my fastest technique.

A further combination using osoto-gari came about completely by accident which is often the case at first. It happened one day when, during practice, I went for osoto-gari but changed my mind. As I withdrew from this attack, I turned my body in the opposite direction and found to my astonishment that my opponent couldn't help falling over the other way. From this 'accident', I developed an osoto-gari into hiza-guruma combination. If, in pressing home my right osoto-gari, I find my opponent defends by transferring his weight onto his left leg, I feint osoto-gari and, just where he transfers his weight and before my right leg has completed its entry, I hop back onto my left leg, simultaneously twisting my body to the right and planting my right foot firmly below his left knee, thus causing him to wheel over his blocked, supporting left leg. Taking an initially high lapel grip for osoto-gari enables me to slip my hand over my opponent's back to achieve a stronger wheeling action for the hiza-guruma.

At this time, however, I continued working on two techniques that I had begun earlier but were not quite succeeding – one standing and one groundwork technique. It was in the late 1970s that the yoko-tomoe-nage throw, developed earlier by the Japanese, was coming into its own in Europe and from the start I was attracted by its effectiveness, particularly as my increased confidence on the ground allowed me to do dropping or sacrifice throws. The beauty of yoko-tomoe-nage compared with the traditional method of throwing your opponent over your head, is that you can throw your opponent in any direction he wants to go (generally to one side) and it also works as a perfect combination into tate-shiho-gatame. Instead of using your right foot with a right-handed grip and throwing your opponent over the top, you use your left foot for the throw and simply tip them sideways off your leg. There are many variations of this technique, but I favour dropping my left shoulder towards my opponent's feet as he moves towards his right front corner, so that he is thrown in that direction. The action of my left hand is very important for executing the pull across my opponent's body which results in him 'tipping' off my leg.

The groundwork technique I continued to study was sangaku-jime which was the leg strangle Gilbert had caught me with in 1978. I may have started to work on it to make doubly sure that I would never be caught by it again, but the more I looked at it, the more I could see links with my juji-gatame roll. There are many variations of the rolling juji-gatame but I particularly favour those which allow me to employ the strength in my legs to turn my opponent. But if my opponent is particularly strong at defending juji-gatame, I remove my left leg from behind his left knee, having already secured a firm grip on his left wrist, and swiftly twist my body 180 degrees to a position in which I am virtually sitting on and controlling my opponent's head. I force my left leg under my opponent's right arm and underneath his body and proceed to use his left arm as a lever to pull him over and on top of me. With my left leg now lying straight across the side of his neck, the sangaku-jime falls into place like a jigsaw when my right leg moves across to trap his right arm and my right foot hooks behind the back of my left knee. Reaching across and pulling his right arm firmly against the side of his neck then ensures that, once my legs start to squeeze together, a submission can be obtained.

It was with this armoury that I approached the World Championships in Maastricht in September 1981. I had never felt better, either technically (most of my new techniques had had time to settle and become automatic), physically (I was no longer struggling to reduce my weight artificially) and mentally (with no medal in the 1981 European Championships, I didn't feel the pressure of being favourite). And when I look again at the video of my performance, I can see that I fought as well on that day as on any day in my life. I was technically in control, felt confident, was fluent in my movement and determined not just to go out and win but to go out and win well. And I was able to reap the rewards of the work I had put in. The big uchi-mata, tai-otoshi, kouchi-gari, osoto-gari, yoko-tomoe-nage and my hold-downs all contributed to a smooth passage to the final against Kase. Once there, and once on Kase's back, I was able to prove to myself that I had systematically studied the armlock from the first tentative steps to advanced level, and I had done it by myself. My long days of apprenticeship were over.

10

STAYING AT THE TOP

Everyone wants to beat the World Champion yet there is no shame in losing to him. Everyone studies the World Champion more acutely than anyone else in their weight category for he is the most important stepping stone of all. They watch him fight in contest and they watch videos of his favourite movements again and again. When they go out to fight him, they are aware that however popular a figure he may be, it takes only one brave, little move on the part of the challenger and the crowd is roaring for the success of a giant killer.

If the World Champion has a reputation for dispatching opponents skilfully, mostly with full points, then the challenger does well to last the course. He can afford to come into a contest bent over double in defence, determined that whatever happens, he will take the World Champion to time without score even if, by following these tactics, there is no possibility of him winning the fight. The greater the reputation of the World Champion, the greater the reflected glory of the opponent who has managed to last five minutes without being thrown for full point, submitting or being held-down. This also means the greater the consequent pressure on the World Champion. It doesn't matter whether he is European or Japanese, whether he is Neil Adams or Yamashita, Coe, Cram or Carl Lewis, the pressure is the same. Yet at top level, the difference between the gold, silver and bronze positions from the point of view of technical standard is often very small. Occasionally, Coe and Cram will streak ahead opening a 20-metre gap, but more often than not there is less than a metre or two between the first three or four. As no man is infallible, the current gods of the track sometimes have off-nights or make a tactical error which despite their normal superiority leaves them well down in the field.

In judo this closeness in technical ability often results in apparent stalemate. So often it seems, particularly in a final, that two men supposedly met in fierce combat are doing nothing but shuffling around like a couple of bulls with their horns locked. In one way it is like two runners travelling side by side for the majority of the race until one just edges in front at the right moment. However, in judo it is far more complex. It may be that in a final there is a challenger who is just content to last the time and wants to stop any of the Champion's big attacks stone dead. It would not be difficult to contain most of the top fighters by carefully studying videos and doing specific strength training.

On the other hand, if that final has brought together two judoka of equal stature, then the contest may be a more rarefied one where the battle is one of wills which manifest themselves through the tactical, chess-like fight for dominant grips. Although sometimes tedious to the uninformed audience, this can be as exciting to the practised eye as half-a-dozen failed throws or groundwork moves.

I had started to become a marked man by the end of the 1970s but the pressure really began after Maastricht. I could tell that young opponents were coming out to fight me having done their homework on me just as I had done on my predecessors. They knew my style almost as well as me. They knew that I liked to feel settled with my grip before launching an attack and that that meant gripping my opponent's high left collar or back of his left shoulder as well as obtaining a good hold on his right-hand sleeve. They knew I was strong on the ground so it was imperative that they stay away from groundwork and especially the armlock or sangaku-jime. They knew that if I did get my grip, they had to make a flurry of attacks, however meaningless, in an attempt to break my grip and stop me countering. This way, they might last until the bell. And I could tell that they had watched videos of my movements until they could replay them in their minds, enabling them to read me like a book – or so they thought.

There were difficulties on my side, too. I had been successful with my repertoire of throws and groundwork and it was only too tempting to rely on the old favourites which still worked against most opponents I faced and I wasn't likely to get countered by the others even if the techniques were not going to score so highly. Was the effort and the danger of developing and trying new techniques and combinations worth it? The answer, or course, had to be yes, and yet as 1982 dawned, I had no idea how much my judo was going to change.

Although this will seem strange to many who have followed my competition career over the past years, I feel I have changed almost as much in the years since Maastricht as in those apprenticeship years from 1975 to 1981. There was a change in personal attitude which was perhaps inevitable with a world title behind me and was also a result of getting older for I was less cocky and arrogant than before.

More crucially, there was a change in my whole attitude towards competition. Since being a junior I had revelled in the performance side of judo, playing to crowds with big throws or dramatic armlocks. As I became more experienced, however, I adopted a more professional approach to contests. I was not there to entertain or to put on a show but to get that ippon. Like sprinters learning to run in three-feet wide tunnels on the track, paying attention only to their technique and almost unaware (but not quite!) of their competitors, I concentrated more on the job in hand. At least, that was the ideal I was working towards even though, sometimes frequently, outside pressures interfered with that concentration.

I did more groundwork because that became the most efficient way to achieve ippon. And, equally important, I learned to play a waiting game. As a challenger, I always took the initiative and rarely countered. I preferred to dominate the grips and launch the attacks rather than allow a free for all to see what developed. I moved around a great deal but it wasn't always to my advantage as I probably missed a few positive techniques I could have done by just attacking indiscriminately.

However, after Maastricht, I was more prepared to accept wins by smaller scores. If the big throw wasn't there and my opponent would run off the mat as soon as we got to the ground, then I was more ready to win on decision or koka. Sometimes, I played the rules too closely and lost fights I should never have lost because a referee interpreted a rule differently. But on the whole a more mature approach to competition evolved.

I did not move into 1982, having resumed competitions after admittedly, rather a long rest, with a considered blueprint of my technical future. It is very difficult to produce forward planning like that without the immediate feedback of competition. I had the general aim of making my big techniques, such as tai-otoshi and uchi-mata, a little faster and crisper, making minor adjustments as I went along and adding a few combinations. What I was not prepared for was the disappearance of my tai-otoshi. This is one of the many curious aspects of judo as techniques – mainly standing ones – can just drift away. One moment, they are working well and you are continuing to execute uchi-komi as you have always done and then, little by little, they just start to drift. This happens often during a judo career and there is a danger of panicking, particularly when it affects one of your major techniques. To a certain extent, I had come to terms with this and in 1983 I hardly threw anyone with tai-otoshi, but I didn't worry about it so much because my kouchi-gari and uchi-mata were working and I was doing a lot of groundwork. I continued to do tai-otoshi in training and, perhaps for the first time, allowed one of my favourite techniques which had stopped working for me to come back of its own accord. Usually, techniques do come back and as I write in 1985, my tai-otoshi is working well whereas my uchi-mata has moved into the background. These psychological aspects of judo may not be regarded as important as perfecting a new and wonderful technique, but they are literally half the battle, otherwise the champions would just be top technicians and this is clearly not the case. So my technical development in this most recent phase of my contest career has been stamped not so much by the new standing and groundwork moves that I practised, but rather by how I practised them.

Of course, I did introduce techniques and I am always looking at new moves because I get a kick out of adding fresh skills to those I already have. During this period I worked on numerous little variations of juji-gatame and sangaku-jime. I learned one sangaku turn from watching Robert van der Walle, the Belgian former Olympic light heavyweight champion, and I have since used it with some success against opponents who are defending on all fours and blocking my juji-gatame roll. Squatting in front of your opponent, you take the belt in your left hand, and with your left arm and elbow, pull your opponent's head towards the ground. You place your right knee at the side of his face and slip your left foot into the same gap as the previously described sangaku, behind the opponent's right arm. By tipping your opponent forward and to one side, it is possible to squeeze your own legs together, move into a sangaku position, tie up his left arm and proceed into the armlock, strangle or hold. It is simple, but effective.

Incidentally, Kashiwazaki couldn't believe the high percentage of successful armlocks used in competition in this country, which was even reflected in British competitors' success abroad not only by me but also by Steve Gawthorpe and Neil Eckersley in the European Championships and the Olympics in 1984. But by Olympic year it became clear to me that it was time to redress the balance because while developing the armlock, we had neglected hold-downs. Following Kashiwazaki's example, a number of boys in the squad started to incorporate techniques such as obi-tori-gaeshi into their repertoires.

Another useful technique which Kashiwazaki taught was how to extricate your leg when you are virtually in mune-gatame and lying on the left side of your partner with your right leg trapped. First of all, it is important to tie up your partner's right arm, thus immobilising it completely. This is done by inserting your right arm under his elbow and over his forearm and, picking up the bottom of his jacket with your left hand, feeding it into the right. Make sure the whole parcel of arm and jacket is tight. With your partner's top half now secure (controlling his head with the back of your shoulder) you can turn your attention to his legs.

With your left hand, reach down and grasp the cloth at your opponent's right knee and be ready to pull as, with your left foot placed against your

Katsuhiko Kashiwazaki (Japan) won the 1981 U65k world title in Maastricht, Holland through his meticulous groundwork. Here he is methodically extricating his leg and holding the Romanian Constantin Nicolae

partner's left knee, you begin to push. The simultaneous pull and push action should release the captured leg. Like most moves in groundwork, it is important to complete one step at a time rather than rush in and try to do everything at once.

My natural affinity with armlocks was confirmed because while I worked on this slick manoeuvre, my attention naturally turned towards armlock possibilities. If, at the start of the move, your opponent resists bending his arm to allow you to tie it up, you can apply a straight armlock in an entwined manner by putting your right forearm under his elbow, fingers grasping your right wrist and your left hand grasping his wrist. If he bends his wrist just a little way, you can then entwine the arm in a similar fashion, sit him up, and take the arm backwards for the armlock. But don't let him bend his arm and grasp his judogi. When you consider the number of times you are caught in this basic position, with one leg trapped, it is worth spending six months practising freeing the leg and looking for other possibilities from that position apart from the armlock. And exactly the same applies when you are lying on your back with your opponent between your legs. All Dan grades should have four or more moves that they can easily execute from the basic positions: when your opponent is on all fours or between your legs; or when you are in between his legs or your leg is trapped. You would be ill advised to go into an all-fours position yourself except in an absolute emergency.

In the two years before the Los Angeles Olympics, I had continued to work hard on the yoko-tomoe-nage despite not having conspicuous success with it in competition, when suddenly it started to work. I was doing much the same as I always had: from a right-hand grip, I put my left foot into my opponent's stomach or against his hip and fiercely pull his right-hand sleeve to throw him over my left shoulder. At first, I used to go down to the ground and my opponent would collapse on top of me, but in about 1983, I began to bring my right foot up as well to turn him over even more and that seemed to work very effectively. Both Nowak and Lescak fell victim to that technique in Los Angeles, and now I know I can rely on it, particularly when I concentrate on a strong left-hand pull which has been such an important part of all my throws. Although the yoko-tomoe-nage really began to work while Kashiwazaki was at the Budokwai, my technique was strangely more akin to the throw which Fuji, the great middleweight who retired just before I started seriously to compete, used to do when he stopped morote-seoi-nage, again after an injury.

On useful tip I learnt from Kashiwazaki was his footsweep. I had always done a kind of double footsweep, when I used to take the further leg, but I did find Kashiwazaki's method of hooking onto the leg and taking it as the opponent tried to step off it very interesting. The first time it worked effectively for me was in the European Championships against Myllyla, and now again it is something that I can safely attempt at most times. I have my favourite uchi-mata grip in which my right hand firmly holds the top of my opponent's left shoulder, and I use it not only to throw but also to open up defensive opponents for an attempt at uchi-mata.

The work I did on the footsweep or foot hook as it really is, combined with the years of work I had done on my kouchi-gari, paid unexpected dividends in the 1984 European Championships against the Frenchman Michel Nowak. After enduring a couple of minutes of the usual bruising and battering he hands out, I swiftly stepped to the left and, instead of applying a kouchi on his right foot in the normal manner, my right foot connected with his advancing left foot and I levelled him with a spectacular footsweep which was one of the best I have ever done.

The many unpredictable factors in judo make it difficult to plan the development of new techniques in minute detail. You may be attracted to a throw and work on it assiduously for a year, but in the end, find that it just doesn't suit your individual body movement. Conditioning work, however, can be mapped out with a far greater degree of certainty that the desired result will be reached. If my post World Championship period has been marked by anything, it has been by the much more methodical physical preparation I have done. This was made possible, in part, by a conscious decision to enter fewer contests during the year. Even before 1981, I was reducing my contests from the one every five weeks or so which I had been taking part in during the late 1970s, but after Maastricht I preferred in general to concentrate on the big events, with some warm-up contests when I felt necessary, rather than enter everything in sight.

This spacing of contests allowed me to work on my conditioning in a much more scientific way, as well as enabling me to peak for the big events. And my change in fighting attitude from the youthful and impulsive all-action style to a more circumspect approach was matched by a dramatic physical change. Between 1982 and the 1984 pre-Olympic period, I nearly doubled my strength factor.

My decision to start on a heavy weights programme was prompted by the fact I found I was being out-strengthed by fighters like Nowak and the Russian Shota Khabarelli. I felt that the only reason these judoka were able to compete against me was because of their sheer power. So, given my level of skill, if I could be as strong as they were, I would beat them. To be honest, I don't like working heavy weights because it is painful, but I felt the practice was necessary. Although most top judo competitors use weights, few even now use them as methodically as I do, yet what was to emerge as a carefully-planned programme and an integral part of my whole conditioning work took time to develop. But I am happy with the so-called triple phasing that I do today.

Triple phasing starts with a base training which is concerned with developing the basic fitness and stamina you need to train. You simply cannot concentrate on the complex technical aspects of judo if you are having difficulty in standing up straight after an hour of practice. Base training involves distance work. I do longer runs than usual, four or maybe five miles, followed by cardio-vascular circuits which are geared to training the heart and include skipping or cycling.

A normal day during my base training period is as follows: I get up at about 8 a.m. and start running at about 11 a.m. I run a 4½-mile route in about 25 minutes and then rest for half an hour. Then I do what I call the 'Blast' which entails 20 minutes of skipping, 20 minutes on the running machine and 20 minutes on another similar exercise machine. That is one hour of hell. It is followed by a body circuit – sit-ups, press-ups, squat

Technique against strength – getting to grips with the muscle power of Michel Nowak – at the 1982 European Championships in Rostock, East Germany. So far, technique has always prevailed

jumps, burpees and others – on one day and a cardio-vascular weights circuit – light weights with many repetitions – the next. Both consist of six exercises and I will do three series of those six exercises without rest. Then it is followed by 30 minutes of stretching.

The afternoon is devoted to whatever bits of 'work' arise, such as promotional work with one of my sponsors, and then I do an hour and a half of judo in the evening. One day a week, sometimes two, I reduce the conditioning training and go into the dojo with my training partner for some skill work when we look at new ideas and polish up old ones. I follow this pattern from Monday to Friday and rest on Saturday and Sunday. I used to train six days a week but now I realise that rest is very important and I will train for five days only; neither will I train through injury or illness.

I follow the base training routine for three weeks to a month, depending on when my next competition is scheduled for, and then move on to the next section which is the power phase. During this, I do shorter runs, perhaps two miles at about the same time each morning, followed by a 30-minute 'Blast', consisting of 10 minutes' skipping, 10 minutes' cycling and 10 minutes on a running machine. I then follow it by power weights.

I pyramid my weights which means that I build up my weights to a maximum, starting off with ten on each exercise, followed by eight, then six, then four. Then I start to decrease the repetitions and increase the weight, which makes it harder. I practise a variety of lifts, each one for some judo purpose. I do cleans, locking to the forearm and locking to the stomach. I do reverse curls, a lot of lats and triceps work and bench press. When I started I couldn't bench press 200 lb but I can do 280 now. I warm up with 200. I also do a lot of hanging from bars which gives the same effect as pulling in judo.

This heavy work is always followed by stretching and then by judo. I try to keep the judo just a bit lighter than normal because I feel fairly exhausted. Heavy weights always result in a slight deterioration in my judo, because I lose the movement in my legs – in fact, they can become quite dead. But the slowing up is only temporary. Once again, I will occasionally insert a skill session in place of an afternoon of weights, partly to make my programme more interesting and partly as an escape from the tedium and the pain.

Early morning press-ups at Crystal Palace with my dog, Bob

The power phase again lasts for about three weeks to a month and then I move on to the local endurance period. This consists of a three-mile run, sometimes a little more, or what I call 'wind sprints'. I do a 60-metre sprint against the wind, if possible, and then jog back to the start and do it again. I will probably do ten of those before arriving at the gym. I'll do ten minutes of skipping followed by local endurance circuits. I do the same set of six body circuit exercises as before, but this time I will do three sets of a particular exercise before moving on to the next one. This enables you to overload specific areas of your body.

Then, in the evening, it is judo again, but now I concentrate on certain techniques. By this time, it is drawing closer to an event and the physical conditioning must almost be completed. I will then go into a short-speed phase just before the contest, which consists of no weights, some shuttle running in the morning, body circuits, lots of stretching, and just concentrating on judo. I do a lot of fast uchi-komi, and some light judo, and as much throwing practice as I can get. Then, nearer the event, I start to taper off, so that I stop completely four or five days before the competition.

By this time, I should be at a peak of physical fitness and my judo should be extremely sharp. In effect, I have 'peaked' but I find it very difficult to organise my training so that I peak on a certain day. Normally, I can hit my peak over a two-week period but sometimes I reach it too soon. In 1983, for instance, I peaked at the British Open in April though I had intended to do so for the European Championship in May. I wasn't bad in Paris but not as good as I had been at Crystal Palace the previous month. However, even without peaking, there is, of course, a minimum standard beneath which I will not fall, regardless of my preparation and that, I suppose, is because of the years of top-class competition.

Most of my work in the gym is done with a training partner. Since May 1982 I have worked with Ray Stevens who came second to me in the Trials that year and who is now one of the leading U86k players in the country. After years of this kind of work, you do need help sometimes in motivating yourself, both to get down to training and to train well – it is no good just going through the motions. People who do judo for fun do not understand what it is like to train for three or four hours during the day and still try to be fresh in the evening judo session. But if you have a good, consistent training partner, you can help one another over the rough times when the weights are beginning to hurt and laugh over the times when the training is so boring that you are getting really fed up.

From the point of view of developing judo skills, a good training partner is imperative. I don't entirely agree with the Japanese sempai/kohei system, where the junior student, the kohei, is at the beck and call of the sempai. I mean, if I told Ray to go and wash my kit, he would tell me where to go – and quite rightly too. We are different from the Japanese. But you do need someone with whom you can work as a team, learn to adapt to each other's body shape and movement and develop a smooth and useful uchi-komi routine. If you do uchi-komi with an orange belt, the arms and legs are all in the wrong place and you end up hitting him at the wrong angle. For me, that kind of uchi-komi is a waste of time. Yet good uchi-komi is crucial for it is the basis of your judo skill. Without being able to do good uchi-komi – and I was surprised to find that most of the young boys coming into the National Senior Squad could not do it well even on their favourite throws and moves – you cannot develop techniques. You start on new techniques with uchi-komi, which enables you to break down the move into its basic parts and learn to understand the mechanics of the throw and then gradually introduce them in the evening judo session, starting on the lower grades and gradually working your way up. I always measure myself against certain people, for instance, Paul Ajala at the Budokwai is one of the top three or four in the U71ks and if I can't throw him, then I know there is something wrong with my judo. Perhaps I am tired or stale, or the weights programme has been slowing me down. So I know I must change my training slightly and perhaps have a skill session on the mat. I get feedback from judoka like Paul who will perhaps say that he was able to block me more than he should have, either standing or on the ground, or that I felt particularly strong or fast.

It is inevitable that the physical changes achieved through my triple-phasing programmes have altered my judo, though age has much to do with it too. At 27, I do not move around the mat in the same way I used to at 20. But I think my speed of entry into a throw is just as fast and that is the important thing. It is not how many times you attack in a contest that matters but if, when you make one really positive attack you can explode into it, and yet still execute it correctly. That is why I am not so much in favour of speed uchi-komi, where you try for an artificially high number of attacks at the expense of all the important details that actually make a technique work. Quality, not quantity, is important rather like in the judo sessions. It makes more sense to me to fight a good 90 minutes in England rather than hanging on for a grim three hours in Japan.

In any case, staying at the top is very different from pulling yourself up the rungs of the ladder. If you reach the top with a solid technical base, then staying there is largely a question of motivation, keeping fit (judo competition is basically a young man's sport) and keeping a fresh and open mind about the technical side of judo. After all, it is the Champions who create the fashions but the danger of being trapped in a technical rut or becoming too obsessed with physical conditioning is only too great. Maintaining the correct mental attitude is probably the most difficult aspect of all.

What will happen technically to my judo over the next few years is impossible to say – for a start, so much will depend on whether I continue competing. As I write, I am working on Russian-style pick-ups that may eventually become part of my contest judo or which I may find, after some months, do not really suit me. All I can hope is that even after my competition days, I will never lose the enjoyment I get even now of developing something new or seeing something unusual on the judo mat. Although I have worked hard on my conditioning, raising that to a level of a skill, I am first and foremost a judo man and bench-pressing 300 lb gives me nowhere near the same level of satisfaction as a cracking uchi-mata executed in the white-heat of contest.

GLOSSARY

Ashi-barai	Sweeping ankle
Ashi-waza	Ankle technique
Budo	Martial way
Bushido	The way of the warrior
Chui	Five point penalty
Dan	A step. There are 12 Dan grades of proficiency, the first five of which are black belts
Do	Way or path
Dojo	Training hall
Eri	Collar or lapel
Hadaka-jime	Naked strangle
Hajime	Begin
Hane-goshi	Spring hip throw
Hansoku-make	Disqualification through breaking contest rules
Hara	Stomach
Harai	Sweeping
Harai-goshi	Sweeping loin throw
Hidari	Left
Hiki-wake	A draw in contest
Hiza-guruma	Knee wheel throw
Ippon	Full point in contest, equivalent to ten small points
Ippon-seoi-nage	One arm shoulder throw
Jigotai	Defensive posture
Ju	Gentle in the sense of yielding
Judo	The gentle way
Judoka	Traditionally, a high-grade exponent of judo

Juji-gatame	Straight armlock
Juji-jime	Normal cross strangle
Ju-jitsu	The gentle art and the original self-defence system from which judo emerged
Ju-no-kata	The demonstration of techniques of gentleness
Kaeshi	Counter
Kaeshi-waza	Counter throw
Kake	Act of throwing
Kami-shiho-gatame	Hold-down by controlling upper four quarters
Kani-hasami	Scissors throw
Kansetsuwaza	Lock technique
Kappo	Resuscitation technique
Karate	Empty hand – art of punching and kicking
Kata	Pre-arranged form
Kata-gatame	Shoulder hold
Kata-garuma	Shoulder wheel
Kata-ha-jime	Single wing strangle
Kata-juji-jime	Half cross strangle
Katame-waza	Groundwork technique
Kesa-gatame	Scarf hold
Keikoku	Penalty equivalent to seven small points
Ki	Psychophysical energy
Kodokan	Hall for studying the Way
Koka	Smallest score, equivalent to three small points
Koshi	Hip
Kosoto-gake	Minor outer hooking
Kosoto-gari	Minor outer reaping
Kouchi-gari	Minor inner reaping
Kouchi-gake	Minor inner hooking
Kuzure-kame-shiho-gatame	Broken upper four quarters hold
Kuzushi	Break balance
Kyu	To seek or to study

Maki-komi	Winding technique
Migi	Right side
Morote-seoi-nage	Double hand shoulder throw
Morote-gari	Double hand clip
Mune-gatame	Chest hold
Nage-no-kata	Demonstration of throwing techniques
Name-juji-jime	Normal cross strangle
Newaza	Groundwork
Obi	Belt
Obi-tori	To hold the belt
O-goshi	Major hip throw
O-guruma	Major wheel throw
Okuri-ashi-barai	Sweeping ankle throw
Okuri-eri-jima	Sliding collar strangle
Osaekomi	Holding
Osoto-gari	Major outer reaping
Ouchi-gari	Major inner reaping
Randori	Free practice
Rei	Bow
Renraku-waza	Combination techniques
Ryu	Method or style or school
Sasae-tsuri-komi-ashi	Propping drawing ankle throw
Sensei	Teacher or instructor
Seoi	Shouder
Seoi-nage	Shoulder throw
Seoi-otoshi	Drop shoulder throw
Shiai	Contest
Shido	Warning – smallest penalty in contest (three points)
Sode-tsuri-komi-goshi	Sleeve lifting hip throw
Sukui-nage	Scoop throw
Sutemi-waza	Sacrifice throw
Tai	Body

Tai-otoshi	Body drop throw
Tani-otoshi	Valley drop throw
Tatami	Judo mat
Tate-shiho-gatame	All-fours holding
Te-waza	Hand technique
Uchi-komi	Repetition
Uchi-mata	Inner thigh throw
Ude-garami	Entangle armlock
Ude-kujiki-juji-gatame	Straight armlock
Uke	Receiver – person being thrown
Ukemi	Breakfalls
Uki-goshi	Floating hip throw
Ura-nage	Rear throw
Waki-gatame	Armpit armlock
Waza	Technique
Waza-ari	Seven small points in contest
Waza-ari-awazeti-ippon	In contest, a second waza-ari equals ippon
Yame	Stop
Yoko-shiho-gatame	Side four quarters hold
Yuko	Five small points in contest
Yusei-gachi	Referee's term declaring win on superiority
Zen	Meditation, school of Japanese and Korean Buddhism
Zori	Sandals

CAREER HIGHLIGHTS

1969	British Junior Champion
1970	British Junior Champion
1971	British Junior Champion
1972	British Junior Champion
1973	British Junior Champion
1974	Espoir Trials Champion Espoir European Champion U58K
1975	Espoir European, Bronze U65K Junior European, Bronze U71K
1976	All-England Champion Junior World Championships, Bronze British Open Championships, Silver
1977	Junior European Champion Senior European Championships, Bronze All-England Champion British Open Champion
1978	British Open Championships, Silver Senior European Championships, Bronze British Closed Championships All England Champion
1979	British Open Champion U78K European Champion World Championships, Bronze
1980	British Open Champion U78K Swedish Open Champion U78K American Open Champion U78K European Champion U78K Hungary Cup Champion U78K Moscow Olympics, Silver U71K
1981	American Open Champion U78K British Open Champion U78K World Champion U78K

1982	British Open Champion European Championships, Bronze Awarded the MBE
1983	British Open Champion European Champion British Masters Champion World Championships, Silver
1984	British Open European Champion Los Angeles Olympics, Silver
1985	West German Open Champion British Open Champion European Champion World Championships, Bronze